Water Bears

DAVID K. REYNOLDS, Ph.D.

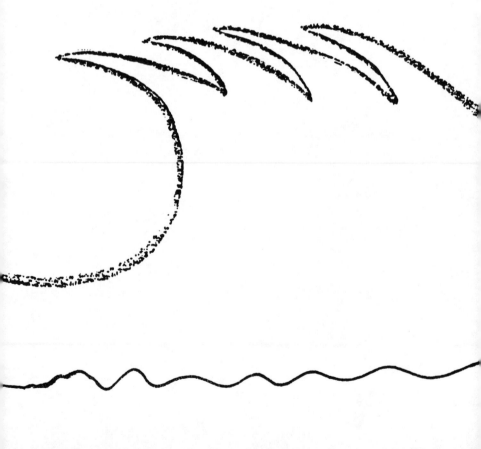

No Scars

JAPANESE LIFEWAYS
FOR PERSONAL GROWTH

QUILL

WILLIAM MORROW NEW YORK

All rights reserved. No part of this book may be reproduced or utilized in any form or by any means, electronic or mechanical, including photocopying, recording or by any information storage and retrieval system, without permission in writing from the Publisher. Inquiries should be addressed to Permissions Department, William Morrow and Company, Inc., 105 Madison Ave., New York, N.Y. 10016

Library of Congress Cataloging-in-Publication Data

Reynolds, David K.
    Water bears no scars.
    Bibliography: p.
    1. Morita psychotherapy. 2. Naikan psychotherapy.
I. Title.
RC489.M65R53 1987   616.89´14   87-7036
ISBN 0-688-07448-0 (pbk.)

Printed in the United States of America

BOOK DESIGN BY MARIA EPES/PANDORA SPELIOS

This book is dedicated to Dr. and Mrs. Mamoru Iga—mentors, patrons, friends.

Preface

We live in an era of leisure. Technologically advanced countries allow a freedom from life-threatening insecurity never before found in the history of humankind. Without the purpose of the struggle for everyday survival we find increasing numbers of people drifting into lethargy, drugs, suicide.

It isn't necessary to work as hard, or sometimes even to work at all to survive. The psychological effects of this lack of meaningful activity are disturbing. There has come a slow shift from doing something worthwhile to just filling time. Those who are just putting in the hours of their lives are nearly dead already. The essays in this book are about a lifeway that can underlie and make meaningful both work and leisure activities. This lifeway focuses on the quality with which an act, even a simple act like washing dishes or dialing a telephone, is carried out. It turns every moment's behavior into an exercise in character development and growth. We need not wait for big events and others' decisions to determine who we are. The opportunity to become who we want to become lies in this very moment's behavior.

Conditions of modern life leave us much time to do as we please, and as much or as little as we please. The gut-level meaning involved in the hunt or the gathering of crops or the creation of hand tools or the learning of survival techniques has been replaced by dependence on specialists, professionals who grow and process our food, create our clothing and houses for us, teach us remote and impractical information in our schools. If there is to be meaning in shopping, baseball, movies, and adult education, then it must be found on a level different from the face-to-face encounter with survival.

The lifeway that I have been writing about creates meaning on another level, a level that has nothing to do with the intrinsic value of any particular activity. The focus on the quality of action applies as well to tying one's shoelaces as to performing surgery. Therein lies its value. One need not be chairing the board of a large corporation or running a branch of the government or performing before thousands of fans; one need not even be able to leave one's hospital room or one's bed, or be able to see or hear in order to find purpose and meaning in everyday life.

This volume is the third in a series on the use of Eastern lifeways and personal-growth methods in the West. In *Playing Ball on Running Water* (and, elsewhere, in *Constructive Living*) I began to outline the ways in which Moritist and Naikan ideas from Japan could be of concrete, practical use in a program of self-development. In *Even in Summer the Ice Doesn't Melt* these ideas and exercises were extended and deepened. Now, in *Water Bears No Scars,* new stories, illustrations, and exercises will build the student's understanding and practice yet further.

The water theme flows through all the titles in this series. Water has the quality of nonresistance to its containers, its boundaries; yet it constantly pushes toward its goal. Its patience and persistence are examples for us. And when the time and circumstances are ripe, water rushes toward its destination in rapids and waterfalls. The situational appropriateness of the flow of water is well considered in Eastern literature. The water images from Buddhist and Taoist koans and verse were adapted for these book titles.

Acknowledgments

People on both sides of the Pacific helped me learn and develop this constructive-living method. The director of Seikatsu no Hakkenkai, Yozo Hasegawa, taught me by his words and his actions about this lifeway. Dr. Hiromu Shimbo and his family showed me unflagging courtesy and hospitality during my annual stays in Japan. The staff members at the Hakkenkai office and the board of directors gave concrete support and encouragement.

The Tamashiros and Ogawas on their respective islands of Kauai and Maui provided living models of constructive lifestyles, allowing me to live with them as I learned and wrote.

My wife, Lynn, exhibits her wonderful steadiness and patience through my isolated periods of writing and travel. She keeps on teaching me dependability and responsibility.

At Morrow, Douglas Stumpf and his assistant, Barry Schwabsky, provide just the right balance of distance for independent freedom and closeness for supportive encouragement.

Somehow, books get written. Looking back I sometimes wonder how and who, but never why.

Contents

The shadow of the bamboo sweeps the steps,
　　But the dust does not stir;
The moon's disc bores into the lake
　　But the water shows no scar.

—From the Taoist *Saikondan*

ᴎᴧᴧᴧᴧᴧᴎ
ᴎᴧᴧᴧᴧᴧᴎ
ᴎᴧᴧᴧᴧᴧᴎ

Weeds

PERSPECTIVE

This morning I have been weeding a wonderfully instructive garden on the island of Kauai. It is the size of a house lot and contains a wide variety of vegetables and fruits and flowers. I spend many hours each year working in this garden. It has taught me quite a few lessons that extend beyond its ti leaf boundaries.

Today, as I weeded among the cabbage, lettuce, and chrysanthemums, I was struck by the necessity of looking for the little green interlopers from many different angles. After it appeared that I had cleared a bed of weeds, I could walk back around it and find a number that had been missed—some as big as my hand. Another circuit of the patch at a different angle, with a few leaves pulled out of the way, and I could find still more weeds to be cleared.

It's very unlikely that the latter had sprung up suddenly in the few minutes since the last round of weeding. They were there all along, unseen. The different angle of the sun and the shift of the wind helped make them visible. It was the combination of the changing circumstances and my changing perspective that brought them to light.

I'm glad that I took the time to go over the same ground a

couple of extra times. There was something to learn from doing so. Probably, there are still a few weeds hiding among my leafy friends. That's all right. I have to decide when there is something more important to do than going over those beds again. The weeds I missed will grow larger and more visible with time. Someday I'll catch them and leave some others.

The line between thoroughness and unconstructive perfectionism is one we may draw and cross every day. The garden reminds me of that line. It reminds me, too, of what psychotherapy ought to be about in contrast to what it has, all too often, become. There comes a time when it is no longer useful to go over the same ground again. It is time to be planting new beds.

PERSISTENCE

Weeding doesn't show results in the same way that planting does. After we have weeded for a few hours, the result is the absence of something. The effect of weeding is to return the garden or lawn to its proper, previous condition. Planting and harvesting give us something added for our effort. We see green shoots appearing; we have baskets of fruits and vegetables and flowers for our work.

Weeding is thankless, but necessary. It takes diligence and an eye for the value of subtraction to persevere at weeding. The principles of weeding are valuable for all of us, but I especially like to see teachers and students, parents and children, and similar pairs of role groups weeding together.

POSSIBILITY

Here is a modern koan for your consideration:

A friend came over to offer Mrs. Tama help weeding her lawn and garden. The friend appreciated the gifts of fruits from the garden that Mrs. Tama kindly delivered from time to time. Mrs. Tama could use the help, so she gladly accepted his offer.

Day after day the friend put in an hour or two pulling weeds. Unfortunately, there was one variety of clover to which the friend seemed attached. He refused to pull out that clover. Mrs. Tama noticed that the clover remained in the lawn and garden. She pointed out that she considered the clover to be a weed. Nevertheless, the friend continued to let that weed grow while he carefully worked on the other varieties.

The koan, the problem for your consideration here, is "What should Mrs. Tama do?" There are plenty of possibilities for response (or nonresponse). Each one tells us something about Mrs. Tama, and about you. There is only one correct response to this situation. In the real world, Mrs. Tama found it. Can you?

Wisdom

Cleverness isn't the same as wisdom. Wisdom comes with life experience, alertness, and intelligence. Cleverness can be taught, even in classes, even to young people. I think it is not surprising that much of psychotherapy as practiced in the West today is little more than clever conversation. Young people haven't the accumulation of struggles, successes, and failures to advise their clients about living, no matter what degrees they have accumulated.

Let me begin with an example of commonsense advice based on the moral wisdom of Morita therapy: Greet the people you work with and live near when you first encounter them each day. This advice is commonly given to people with difficulties in the social sphere, such as shyness. A recent issue of *Hakkenshi* magazine contained this suggestion. The suggestion is quite simple and straightforward. Whether the person feels isolated or tense or left out or shy or frightened, he is to do the greeting. You may consider that the greeting is merely a behavioral assignment. But it is more than that. It has a moral component.

What the greeting advice is *not* is psychological uncovering by verbal means. By making this assignment we aren't aiming at producing some insight in a psychoanalytic sense. We aren't using words to discover unconscious tendencies. So we are dealing with something quite different from Western verbal encounter therapies.

DAVID K. REYNOLDS

The assignment to greet one's neighbors is built on the recognition that neurosis grows as much from social/moral errors as from wrong understandings and unpleasant feelings (that is, psychological difficulties). The shy person has been neglecting social responsibilities. He has been avoiding simple social courtesies. When he does what is "proper," the social relations are more likely to be smooth and the client is more likely to feel good about them. In the past, when he ignored and avoided people, he felt uncomfortable about them and about himself. The performance of the greeting puts him back on the social track. Whatever the response of others (they may return his greeting or they may snub him), he has done his social part (and has successfully carried out his assignment, as requested). He feels an increased sense of control over the situation. To put it baldly, greetings are "good," "right," "proper," "moral" behaviors.

Morita therapists don't assign just any behaviors when working with clients. They never assign behaviors that are considered "wrong" or "immoral" by society. When they are in doubt about the rightness of a behavior, they leave the choice up to the client or else advise against the behavior. So you see that any "uncrossing of psychological wiring" comes as a result of "correcting" the behavior. And the word "correcting" carries clear moral overtones.

Part of the appeal of Morita therapy to Westerners is that it includes this aspect of moral wisdom. Western psychotherapy has become obsessed with technique. That obsession is partly because Western educators want to train therapists in university settings. We want to teach people intellectually how to guide people out of neurosis. I think it is difficult to teach effective psychotherapy in the classroom to young people with little life experience.

There is nothing wrong with using common sense and wisdom in the psychotherapy setting. So many neurotic difficulties can be solved by straightening out sloppy and thoughtless acts. Morals may not be the same from society to society or from individual to individual, but we cannot neglect the moral side of behavior and avoid psychological consequences.

Some Key Elements of Constructive Living

The English Language Society of the Moritist mental health organization, Seikatsu no Hakkenkai, and I translated a study guide of the key elements of constructive living. In this chapter I have selected some of these basic principles for commentary.

THE VALUE OF SUFFERING

Unpleasant feelings and sensory experiences such as anxiety, fear, pain, and discomfort are disturbing but indispensable to our existence. They remind us of our basic purposes and desires and urge us to action. In contrast, pleasant feelings such as hope, relief, joy, and contentment are less compelling.

Of course, no one is suggesting here that all unpleasant feelings are good and pleasant ones bad. However, many people seem to think that unpleasant feelings have no merit at all. Such people try to erase such feelings with alcohol or tranquilizers or other drugs because they see no useful purpose for them.

A related error is committed by those who focus so much on getting rid of their upsetting feelings that they become distracted from the true purposes to which these feelings are directing them. It is perfectly all right to be fearful, anxious, angry, bored, aroused, indignant, shy, jealous, and so forth. Each of these feelings points us toward some specific desire or purpose that needs to

DAVID K. REYNOLDS

be satisfied or accomplished through constructive activity. We cannot lead a full life without these spurring reminders of what needs doing.

In our constructive life we aim at recognizing and acknowledging all feelings (not just the pleasant ones) and practicing the positive actions that are called for by these feelings. If you are anxious about new job responsibilities, then you want to do well, to succeed at your new tasks. What can you do (action) to prepare yourself for these untried areas of work? How can you go about developing social skills to combat your shyness? What is your timidity telling you about your need for training, for social action, and experience? Grief tells us about the value of someone or something and urges us to repair the holes in the tapestries of our lives created by the absence. Every kind of hurt directs us to some positive self-developing action. Trying to satisfy our associated desires in negative or destructive ways leads only to more unpleasant feelings (such as guilt and remorse), which tell us that the destructive paths are unsatisfying. The original suffering remains.

SOME LAWS OF FEELING

Feelings fade over time if left as they are. When our behavior or our circumstances don't restimulate them, emotions decline in intensity as time passes. This principle applies to love as well as to embarrassment, to confidence as well as to impatience, to joy as well as to terror.

Feelings tend to fade when satisfied or displayed. When we eat, our hunger fades; when we prepare for the business conference, our worries about it diminish; when we verbalize our anger and take action to correct the anger-producing situation, our anger subsides. Certainly, the converse is true—when we fail to eat, our hunger may increase (to a point); when we fail to prepare for the business conference, our anticipatory anxiety increases; when we try to suppress our anger and make no effort to change the anger-producing situation, our anger continues undiminished.

The intensity of a feeling weakens as we become accustomed to it. There is nothing we can do directly to erase an irrational fear of flying (or driving on freeways or speaking in public), but if we continue to fly (or drive on freeways or speak in front of groups) in spite of the fear, we eventually become accustomed to it and experience it as diminished. To flee from unpleasant feelings as soon as they are experienced, either by fleeing from the circumstance or by taking some chemical escape, prevents some people from learning this valuable principle. Living through grief, depression, anger, uncertainty, can produce a confidence in one's ability to endure and persist in positive living.

Feelings are intensified when precipitating stimuli persist and we pay close attention to the feelings. Focusing on feelings may prolong them, particularly when the circumstances that stimulate them reoccur. The more we try to get rid of upsetting feelings directly, the more attention we pay to them, and the more they intensify. It is more effective to leave feelings as they are while we undertake the constructive action that will change our circumstances and indirectly affect our emotions.

Feelings are learned and stimulated by life experiences. There is a vast literature on the ways in which cultural learning molds our emotions. When we are frustrated, we may respond with anger or with fear or with withdrawal or with some other reaction. Reality may limit the kinds of response possible, but we can learn new ways of viewing and responding to the situations in which we find ourselves. We aren't permanently trapped in the mode of, say, fear or anxiety. We learn different emotional responses by putting ourselves in situations where we behave in ways different from our past behaviors, by putting ourselves in new situations, by observing others' responses to situations, by studying ourselves and others. By breaking old patterns of behavior we find new possibilities of emotional response.

Feelings are a kind of natural phenomenon. We have no responsibility for them. What a relief to avoid accountability for one's feelings! Elsewhere in this book I have covered this topic in more detail. Simply put, feelings arise naturally from situations, past experiences, understandings, and behaviors. We have no direct control over them, just as we have no direct control over earthquakes or summer breezes. As our environment changes and as our behavior changes, what we feel changes, too.

On the whole, positive behavior tends to produce and to reinforce pleasant feelings. Conversely, negative behavior tends to produce and reinforce unpleasant feelings. Experiential understanding of this principle can result in a marvelous turnaround in one's life. The words are simple. The day-by-day practice of the principle is much more difficult. Of course, positive behavior doesn't guarantee success in every undertaking—at least in terms of the expected results of the behavior. For example, we can work hard at writing a magazine article and discover that no one wants to publish it. We can develop skills in a job that becomes obsolete with automation. We can work hard at a marriage that turns sour. But the effort involved in the positive behavior is, in itself, rewarding. And, although constructive activity may not guarantee success and good feelings, it increases our chances for joy and satisfaction in a way that negative, destructive activity does not. Violence, pouting, lying, avoiding reality, slander, stealing (others' ideas, time, affection, as well as objects), exploitation, and so forth do not characteristically lead to life satisfaction. I am not intending to be moralistic here. I am simply stating a fact of human existence that anyone can verify by observation and experience.

Negative feelings can be crowded out by positive feelings. Rather than attempting to eliminate worrying, self-doubts, phobias, and the like, a better strategy is to build a constructive lifestyle. The rewards of positive action will take care of the unpleasant feelings.

A feeling-based life is in danger of extreme ups and downs. A purpose-oriented life or a behavior-oriented life is more stable and, in the long run, more satisfying. People who build their lives on feelings are constantly monitoring their feeling state and modifying what they do to try to produce the feelings they hope for. But feelings aren't directly controllable by the will, and they may not be immediately influenced by behavior either. Feeling-oriented people play a risky game at uncontrollable odds. A better payoff in life comes from steadiness in behavior. Let feelings take care of themselves.

* * *

Neurosis is not a disease of the brain or nervous system. It is a learned disorder of the mind. It is built on learned patterns of behavior, unsatisfying attitudes, and misconceptions about reality and the human condition. It can be unlearned.

Highly sensitive people may misconstrue perfectly normal psychological and physical phenomena to be abnormal. Natural and indispensable elements of human existence (such as caution, fear, doubt, reticence, anger, pain, and sadness) are taken to be unnecessary obstacles in their lives. Such people try to eliminate immediate unpleasantness at all cost. They dread suffering, but their attitudes and behaviors only increase their suffering.

They may perceive minor physical complaints such as headaches or dizziness or a pounding heart to be signs of some severe physical disorder in spite of negative results from medical tests. They believe that if only one or two problems in their lives were corrected, all of life would be rosy. They see their physical and psychological problems as absolute weaknesses, external and foreign to them, in need of absolute elimination.

The more they become obsessed with their problems, the greater the problems loom in their minds. They become increasingly aware of the limitations their neurotic habits impose on their lives. As they struggle with their neurotic habits of thought and behavior, they lose track of their larger life purposes as well as their immediate purposes. They become distracted from ordinary living by the struggle with themselves. Escape from suffering becomes their primary life goal.

Our method of constructive living puts the emphasis back on living rather than avoiding or escaping. We learn to take life with all its pleasure and pain. We get busy doing what we know needs to be done in our lives. Some of what we need to do is to change our environments to relieve some of the unnecessary pressures on us. But some pressures we cannot eliminate. (If growing old is bothering you, for example, I know of no way to make you young again.) What we cannot change we must live with as we go about accomplishing our purposes. Special strength comes from enduring unchangeable circumstances while holding to one's purposes.

Some clients in psychotherapy mistakenly believe that verbally expressing their feelings will miraculously dissolve their problems. They believe this falsehood in spite of their experience that the more they complain, the more miserable they feel. I am not advocating the bottling up of all feelings inside without any expression of them. But I am suggesting that talking about feelings or expressing them in action is not a total solution to the problem. When talking becomes complaining, then neurotic habits are reinforced. When we complain, we focus more attention on our suffering and feel it more intensely.

Many suffering people exploit the people around them. They are so caught up in their own misery, they want sympathy and support so much, they are so greedy in their demands on others, that they have little or no awareness of the needs and limitations of those who care about them. In time, their dependency and greediness wears upon their loved ones and workmates. They lament that others don't understand them, that no one suffers as they do. At first they cannot see that the taking, taking, taking is both a result and a cause of their own neurotic pain. They must learn to give themselves away to others and to their purposes if they are to be freed from their self-imposed prison.

Overly sensitive people may not see the positive side of their character. They see the obsession but not the ability to persist. They see the sensitivity to pain but not the potential for sensitivity to others. They see their need for empathy but not their ability to empathize. They see their strong fear of failure but not their strong capacity to succeed. They see their cautious hesitancy to act, but not their imaginative foresight. For each neurotic problem area there is a corresponding positive desire and ability. However, because of their idealism and perfectionism (these qualities, too, have positive aspects) neurotic people focus on the defects and feel inferior. They use their strong analytical powers on themselves in a negative, unproductive manner.

ACCEPTANCE

Acceptance in constructive living has two aspects, a relatively passive aspect and a relatively active one. The passive element involves giving up on trying to change one's immediate feelings in any direct way and avoiding extended fantasies of what might have been or what ought to be. The attitude is one of noticing the feelings and fantasies but taking a "hands off" stance toward them. The active element of acceptance involves constructive action based on the reality that presents itself to us. Reality, too, must be accepted, but we can work to change the circumstances in which we find ourselves. Our efforts must be based on a realistic appraisal of our situation. In both the passive and the active senses acceptance means a sort of broad embracing of what is followed by reality-based effort. There is no fatalistic resignation here, only sensible, practical directed effort.

This approach of acceptance (*arugamama*, in Japanese) cuts into the vicious cycle of attention to suffering and increased sensitivity to cues that remind us of our pain. The focus turns from immediate misery to constructive action. It begins with distraction from suffering, but it leads to reduction of misery through changed behavior and attitudes and changed circumstances as a result of our actions.

This acceptance is more than a method of cure of neurosis; it is a fundamental approach toward life that is useful for anyone. In the spring of 1985 Yozo Hasegawa made an important contribution to theory by pointing out the parallels between obsession with neurotic distress and obsession with work. Thus, he found another bridge to expand the usefulness of our constructive living approach beyond that of the suffering neurotic. The wage earner who goes to work early, returns home late, thinks only about office matters, and scarcely concerns himself with family and community affairs is, in a sense, suffering from a life-narrowing obsession much like that of the symptom-focused neurotic. Any obsession, whether with success or love or control or money or fame or power or a hobby or a car or a promotion or a family or whatever, distracts us from reality. Fixation narrows our attention and turns us away from living fully.

* * *

DAVID K. REYNOLDS

Miserable people are usually feeling-oriented. Much of their thoughts and actions are aimed at producing or reducing certain feelings. They are rarely successful at maintaining comfortable feelings or eliminating uncomfortable ones. In their efforts to do the impossible with feelings, they are distracted from the necessary tasks of everyday life. They judge every action in terms of whether they feel like doing it, what effect it is likely to have on their emotional state, whether it is possible in view of their psychological condition. The balance of their attention is on themselves rather than the task at hand. It is no wonder that they tend to withdraw, avoid, escape—every task begins to look formidable. Simply getting up in the morning or leaving the house may appear insurmountable.

Purpose-orientation is quite another matter. The student of constructive living learns to determine and evaluate behavior in terms of proper purposes and goals. The focus is on what the behavioral effort is intended to accomplish in the real world. No longer do feelings and potential future feelings determine what action will be undertaken. While feeling shy the student undertakes the action of introducing himself. While worrying about the reader's response the student writes the letter of apology. While feeling panicky the student leaves her home to do grocery shopping.

Awareness shifts gradually from the inner state of feelings to the requirements of the surrounding situation. Behavioral successes encourage more attention to the outer world. Experience begins to show that purpose-orientation pays off. What one reads about constructive living makes more sense. One tries more purpose-oriented activity. And so on in a progressing spiral.

The result is usually a great reduction in anxiety and self-doubt, as has been pointed out before. But discomfort won't completely disappear. Nor should it. Anxiety-free living doesn't fit the reality that humans experience. There should be moments of fear and guilt and anxiety and sorrow and trepidation in everyone's life. These feelings are useful in cautioning us about reality. They need not be determinants of our behavior, but they do provide hints about uncomfortable situations and accessory information about what may need to be done.

STEPS TOWARD THE PROCESS OF GROWTH

There is no sudden and complete "conversion" to this lifestyle. The process of growth occurs in fits and starts, painfully and with great effort. Students may find themselves on one or another of the following plateaus for long periods of time. They may move backward temporarily. But the process can never be totally reversed and abandoned once undertaken. Reality demonstrates its long-term value to the student.

Step 1. Students begin to realize that others, too, are suffering from similar problems, thoughts, and patterns of behavior and emotion. They begin to see their problems in constructive-living terms. They begin to doubt their previous views of themselves and of life; they begin to see that they aren't fundamentally different from or inferior to other people. What they thought were crucial weaknesses in their character gradually take on less importance in their thinking.

They begin to communicate more openly with others. They begin to listen to others as well as talking about their own difficulties. The more they hear, the more sense this new perspective makes.

Step 2. The students begin to understand this lifeway more systematically. However, they have trouble putting it into practice on a regular basis. They make efforts to live constructively, but sometimes they forget, escape from reality, doubt the theory and their ability to live by the principles.

Step 3. The students increasingly experience the joy of success obtained from proper action in daily life. The danger at this stage is that they will become attached to the feelings associated with success. When some great effort doesn't result in the expected feelings of accomplishment and joy, the students may be tempted to give up for a while. They are still feeling-oriented. On the whole, though, the vicious cycle of fixated attention and oversensitivity is disrupted. More and more attention is turned outward. The students become less self-protective and clearer about their purposes. Feelings of inferiority diminish.

Step 4. Reality is accepted as it is. A productive life becomes centered around serving others. Reality-oriented, purpose-oriented behavior becomes a habit. Constructive living is no longer considered a set of propositions and principles; it is incorporated naturally into daily life. The students want to share this lifeway with others who wish to learn it. The students go about everyday life with full attention. Feelings are noticed, but feelings no longer are the primary determinants of behavior. A rich existential gratitude emerges.

PRINCIPLES FOR CONSTRUCTIVE LIVING

1. Questions to ask ourselves when anxious and troubled:
   a. What is the immediate problem?
   b. What is the cause of the problem?
   c. What kinds of solutions are there to the problem?
   d. What is the best way I can work a solution?
   e. What prevents me from acting on the solution now?
2. When we undertake something unfamiliar, it is natural to be anxious about it.
3. Actions become habits.
4. We cannot always act with the consistency and skill we desire.
5. There is only one thing that needs to be done in this moment.
6. Absolute perfect action with guaranteed success is impossible to achieve.
7. Worrying about the future is natural but useless.
8. It is possible to rest by shifting from one kind of task to another.

9. Complaining interferes with constructive action and annoys others.
10. Aiming at smaller goals may lead to greater achievements.
11. When behavior is productive and constructive, we are useful to ourselves and to others.
12. Action is newly created moment by moment. It contains and creates our individuality.
13. Questions for self-examination:
    a. How do my views of human existence differ from those listed above? Which views fit my life experience better?
    b. Have I made fruitless efforts in unrealistic directions? How? What needs to be changed?
    c. What are my immediate and long-term goals?
    d. What can I do now to attain my immediate goals?

DAVID K. REYNOLDS

Self-Sacrifice, Service, and Psychotherapy

It may be helpful to spell out the relationship between constructive living and the assignments involving neighborhood cleanup, performing secret services for others, volunteer activities, and the like. If the base of constructive living is focused attention on each moment's experience and activities (knowing one's purpose, accepting feelings, and doing what needs to be done), where is the value of service to others? One could just as easily focus on self-centered assignments, such as cleaning one's own room, treating oneself to a favorite dinner, taking a course in an adult education program. And, of course, the latter assignments are sometimes made, too.

But there is special merit in self-sacrificing service activities for the suffering client. On the simplest level, service to others provides the depressed or anxious student with a distraction from the overwhelming obsession with one's self and one's immediate suffering. The distraction is neither continuous nor permanent. It is intermittent. But it does provide some temporary relief from the preoccupation with "me," "my," and "I." For brief spans of time, the mind that was tuned to the wavelength of the self becomes attuned to others' problems and needs. When feeding the elderly bedridden patient in a nursing home, there are moments when we may take on a perspective somewhat like that of the patient; briefly, we "become" that person. I am not concerned with the debate about whether we can actually see the world through another's eyes or whether we are seeing as we imagine that person to be seeing. In either case, we find some momentary respite from our ordinary view of the world. That opportunity alone is worth the effort.

Second, for the person with a self-image built around being in need of others' help it is important to begin to create a new self-concept that includes the capacity for giving. As I have written elsewhere, we develop our self-image by looking at what we have done in the past. To change our views of ourselves, we must change our pasts. Since we cannot change the past directly, one path open to us is to create a new past by changing what we do now. What we do now becomes our past eventually. When I look back ten years from now, this moment's activity will have become a part of my past, a part that will have some affect on how I see myself ten years from now.

So it is clear that the service assignments aim at creating a certain sort of self-concept. Those who come to me with the greatest resistance to writing letters of gratitude to family members, who believe they have no available energy to create tapes for the blind, who cannot see the point of doing work for someone without getting credit for it, who are too busy to visit at their parents' convenience, are precisely the people who most need to give these assignments a try. I really couldn't argue in some abstract philosophical sense why it is important to be able to see oneself as "one-who-gives" as well as "one-who-takes" from the world. But it is important. Miserable people see themselves as "takers," as burdens or as exploiters of those about them.

The final reason I'll offer here for the tasks of self-sacrifice is that the world deserves such effort. When we look clearly at the efforts of specific people who support us, when we consider the effects of objects and events that permit us to live day by day, when we consider the efforts of our own bodies and minds working so diligently to keep the spark of attention and awareness flickering on our surroundings, then it is only natural to desire to repay the world for our existence. So much happens to us and for us without our conscious action (a heartbeat, for example), our noticing, much less our words of gratitude. There is a method of self-development, called Naikan in Japan, that aims at producing a deeper recognition of what we owe the world. No matter how unfairly we feel we have been treated, no matter how unrecognized our exertion has gone, no matter what limits our bodies and our pasts and our minds have placed on our existence, the balance is overwhelmingly in favor of our deep, continuous, and ongoing-right-now debt to the world. Even as we work to repay the debt, it grows higher. Yet there is no recourse but to try to right the balance.

Again, I cannot argue the case philosophically, but there is something very important about seeing ourselves as people who are working on that existential debt.

Where We Live

Marlene complains that she's not earning thirty thousand dollars a year. Irwin worries because he has no paying job at all. Marge is having trouble with her husband. Larry yearns for that promotion. Does it seem strange that I might ask all of these people how carefully they brushed their teeth that morning? Who cares about brushing teeth when these major life problems appear? Marlene tells me that if she makes more than thirty thousand dollars in a year, she'll take time to clean her teeth with dental floss, too. But right now, there's no time to waste on such hygienic trivialities.

Despite the commercials for toothpaste there is nothing magical about sparkling-white teeth that will attract companions and ensure business success. But those who neglect the details of daily life lose something worth more than thirty thousand dollars. If Marlene does well, with full attention, what life brings to her to do moment by moment, then her salary takes its proper place in perspective. Irwin can find satisfaction in wholeheartedly seeking a job, keeping his appearance neat, even vacuuming the house. Marge will profit from doing her housework well, artfully discussing her dilemma with her husband (whatever he chooses to do about her message), helping the children with their homework, collecting rare coins, finding work outside the home, separating, or whatever she decides needs doing.

Often in life we have no direct control over the outcome of

major events in our lives. Fate or people in authority over us or the aging process or something else may turn an event one way or another. But life continues to present to us "small" events, chances to control the way we turn on a radio, chances to reach gracefully for the soap in the shower, chances to dust and mend and wash dishes well. Each of these "small" events gives us the opportunity to develop our attention and our character infinitesimally. The accumulated effect is powerful and visible, both to ourselves and to others. Larry may never get the promotion, but he can build himself at the office and at home, whether the promotion comes or not, all the while doing his best to lobby for and deserve the promotion that may come his way.

Why try to base life on what may or may not occur? Why evaluate success in terms of something we cannot completely control? Life is built on moment-by-moment doing. Those moments are all we have. The moment of receiving-that-promotion is only one such moment. To be sure, that moment has implications for what life presents to Larry later on, too. But whatever those implications—if he gets a larger office with a window, for example—there will still be only more moments with different challenges, other opportunities to grow or slip back.

Flattery

When I first went to Japan, the flattery there seemed false and even forced. People would praise my Japanese language ability, even though it was clear that there was little enough of it to praise. I felt almost put down, at times, by the contrast between what was obvious reality and what the flatterer was saying. The kind words became a reminder of the less-kind reality. In time, however, I have come to look beyond the content of the flattery to the spirit behind it. It costs a speaker no more energy to say unkind words than it does to say kind ones. The intent is to please, to recognize verbally some effort, to point out some positive tendency. The flattery may be overdone, but the intention of the speaker's effort shouldn't be ignored.

Over the years I have come to overlook the specific content of the flattery and to respect and treasure the spirit that lies behind it. I thank the speaker for his or her kind words, for the thought. Then, sometimes, I go on to state the reality that I see, the reality that appears to me to be at variance with the kind words just spoken. The part of me that thanks the speaker is the Japanese part of me. The part of me that insists on uttering my view of the cooler reality is the American part of me. Something inside insists that it would be a shame to dispense with either side.

DAVID K. REYNOLDS

Preparation and Pace

Most of us can get most of the important things done in our lives most of the time. Once we have actually begun a task, we find it pulls our attention and effort to the end. Often, it's the getting started that is so difficult. Whether the project is painting a wall or a landscape, writing a letter or a book chapter, washing the car or the windows, preparing for the English examination or the IRS, we can find ourselves procrastinating and thus postponing accomplishment.

Now, I have no simple solution to the problem of procrastination. But I do want to suggest that there is a way to ease into a task. My approach to a project is to begin it with a ritualized routine of preparation. There is something about getting into one's running clothes that prepares one for running. Similarly, laying out the watercolors in a particular fashion, filling the water container, setting out the paper in a particular place in a predetermined way, opening the box of watercolors with attention to the aesthetics of the movement (even better, rhythmically grinding the pigments before painting, as some Japanese painters do), always in the same order and with careful attention to each detail—this process prepares the bodymind for painting.

Preparing for a project may not be as intimidating as actually setting to work on it. Meanwhile, the preparation itself focuses the bodymind on the feel of the tools, the look of what needs doing, the smells and sounds that go along with the activity. When preparation is regularized and carried out often enough, it tends to slide one right into the task itself.

Looked at more closely, preparation is not merely a means to smooth our way into a task. Carried out properly, the preparation is itself an element of the practice of constructive living. To prepare well, with full attention, is as important as the spring housecleaning itself or the reorganization of the files or the writing of that note of sympathy. Setting up for a task is part of our program of setting up ourselves to handle what reality brings us with realistic awareness and effort.

Pace, too, deserves our attention. One spring day in 1985, along with a hundred other runners, I entered the Hanapepe Five-Kilometer Run on Kauai. We puffed through old Hanapepe Town and back past the fire station, traversing the loop-course twice to complete the three-plus miles. A few days later I walked the same route. How much I had missed while running!

There are old autos and flower gardens and a whole line of wooden shops with fading paint that I hadn't noticed. There was an irrigation ditch beside the road and quite a few houses that had been there all along, unnoticed.

The pace of walking gave me more time to observe the surroundings. Certainly, I could walk that loop again and make more discoveries. But the running took so much energy and attention that I recalled little more than the surface of the road and the shoes of those running ahead of me.

Single-minded narrow focus can get us where we want to go in the shortest time possible, it seems, and it is appropriate in certain circumstances. But at the cost of the larger view. An occasional stroll helps us get a better perspective on the daily life course in which, too often, we find ourselves racing unnecessarily.

However, there is an important difference between a reasonable pace and procrastination. Frequently I get calls from people who have read one of my books and want to begin individual training. On occasion, I have invited a caller to come for a session the following day. All of the callers preferred to wait a week or two before beginning. They seemed to want time to psyche themselves up for the new undertaking. A conversation might go like this:

"I can understand what you write; it makes sense. But how do I get myself to do it?"

"There's no need to get yourself to do it. Just do it."

"I mean, how can I make myself do what needs to be done?"

"As I said, there's no need to make yourself do what needs doing. Just do it."

"But how can I make myself *want* to do it?"

"It's a waste of time to try to make yourself want to do it. Just do it."

"But I have to make that decision to—"

"No, a decision isn't necessary. Just do it."

" 'Just do it,' you say, but it's not as simple as that."

" 'Just' doesn't mean 'simple.' It means 'only.' "

Perhaps I should remind these callers that we don't change who we are by waiting until it's convenient to do so, until we're psychologically prepared to do so, until we're comfortable about making the changes. I don't want to frighten away the timid ones, though, so they come at their convenience.

Immediate Cure

ELIMINATING THE DUALISM OF MEANS AND END

The possibility of "cure" for neurosis is already present in every suffering person's mind. Constructive living need not be considered a means of achieving freedom from neurotic suffering sometime in the future. It is not merely a method to be used to rid ourselves of unnecessary misery "ultimately." It is about being cured now, in this moment. Living constructively right now *is* cure. The means and the end are the same. My concern for my students is less in their becoming well than in their being well.

There is an interesting parallel here with one of the ideas of Dogen, the famous Zen master. Dogen (1200–1253) denied that sitting in zen meditation was a means that one practiced to achieve enlightenment. He argued that sitting in zazen meditation *was itself* enlightenment. He saw no dualistic split between practicing and achieving some end result.

It is the very same in constructive living. In those moments when we lose ourselves in a constructive activity, our neurotic suffering is gone. My students may undertake an assigned exercise with the intent of working toward personal growth or "cure." However, when they are caught up in composing the letter of apology and gratitude, when they are engrossed in cleaning out the kitchen cabinet, they are no different from anyone whom they would call nonneurotic. In those moments they are free from neurotic suffering. Instant cure. Instant satori.

Such freedom isn't trivial. It is the accumulation of moment after moment of constructive behavior that allows us to call ourselves normal. It is this doing that *is* the distraction from our self-centered merry-go-round of pain. The means is also the end.

ELIMINATING THE DUALISM OF MIND AND BODY

Constructive living through Morita guidance is not a way of training the mind. It is a way of using the bodymind. The doing of a task at hand is not merely an action of the body. It is an action of the bodymind. Morita called this principle *shinshin doitsu* (literally, "mind-body same-one").

Psychology in the West pays lip service to psychosomatic principles, but when we look at Western psychotherapy, we see practices that focus almost entirely on changing mental processes. Yet the physical movement of the body is both a reflection of and a lever for changing the mind. The last sentence is imprecise from our point of view because it makes it appear that changed behavior occurs and then the mind changes. More accurately, changed behavior is already changed mind, and changed mind is already changed behavior. The two are different ways of talking about the same set of phenomena. When was the last time you saw a mind? The concept of "mind" is built on inferences from bodily behavior. An alteration in one *is* an alteration in the other.

Again, we find an interesting parallel from Buddhism in the notion of *sokushin jobutsu* or "enlightenment with this very body." Kukai, the founder of Shingon Buddhism, saw that it makes no sense to talk about the enlightenment of the mind alone or the achievement of some mental Nirvana in the future. The bodymind must participate in any insight or wisdom.

ELIMINATING THE DUALITY OF SUBJECTIVE/OBJECTIVE

There is a famous quote from the Chinese Zen master Ch'ing-yuan (1067–1120):

"Before I had studied Zen for thirty years, I saw mountains as mountains and waters as waters. When I arrived at a more intimate knowledge, I came to the point where I saw that mountains are not mountains and waters are not waters. But now that I have got the very substance I am at rest. For it is just that I see mountains once again as mountains, and waters once again as waters."

I am much indebted to William LaFleur, whose book, *The Karma of Words*, so clearly spells out the Buddhist concepts for which I find these parallels in Moritist thought and practice. LaFleur writes with regard to the above quote:

"It might be said that in Buddhism the problem posed by the symbolizing process of the mind is not unlike that posed by the habitual daydreams, fantasies, and projections that disturb our capacity for 'right seeing.' In a sense, the symbolizing process is itself a digression, a move away from the clear recognition of mountains as merely mountains, waters as merely waters."

Neurotic thinking is filled with the symbolizing that interferes with our seeing what reality presents to us. For example, when anthropophobic people are about to be introduced to someone at a social gathering, their minds are filled with all sorts of symbol baggage. There are memories of past introduction experiences that were embarrassing or anxiety-filled, there are desires to be liked and respected, there are fears of what the other person will be thinking of them, worries about appearance, and so forth. The reality of the person they are about to meet—the face, the clothing, the name, the interests, and words of that person—are likely to be missed because of all the symbolic interference with reality. The mountain is no longer a mountain. It has become a fearful challenge.

In constructive living we aim at being realistic. Of course, no one views reality with total objectivity. We all carry some symbols and selective attention in our encounters with the world before our eyes. But it turns out that as we accumulate constructive life experiences, the mountains look more like mountains and the waters look more like waters.

In our approach to constructive living we recognize that all people have some neurotic characteristics in some moments and all neurotic people have nonneurotic characteristics in some moments. We refuse to view humans in polar categories of normal and neurotic. Each conceptual category contains the other. Tamura Yoshiro pointed out that early Tendai Buddhists in Japan had already discovered that good and evil interpenetrate. These extreme values aren't mutually exclusive; instead, they interpenetrate.

Changing from a primarily neurotic to a generally constructive lifestyle isn't just desirable; it is also terrifying. The Zen master Rinzai wrote that the ordinary person is terrified of transmigration. We are all afraid of extreme change, uncertainty, death, fate, and "getting well." We often choose the familiarity of boredom and suffering rather than the uncertainty of change. What I define as a good or positive change for you may be negative from your perspective.

"The True Man of the Way . . . accepts things as they come . . . when he wants to walk he walks, when he wants to sit he sits; he never has a thought of seeking Buddhahood." Rinzai's words are often quoted. In the same vein, the graduate of the constructive lifeway accepts reality as it comes. When he finds it purposeful to walk, he walks; when he finds it useful to sit, he sits; he never has a thought of seeking (or checking on the progress of) his cure. The parallels are apparent.

From the preceeding examples we can see that the absoluteness of good and bad is lost in the flux of changing circumstance. Is it good to be "normal"? But "normal" contains neurotic moments, too. Is it good to become "cured"? But cure is painful and terrifying. Is it good to walk? to sit? That depends upon the situation, the conditions, what needs to be done. Rather than spending a lot of time and effort trying to come up with an invulnerable structure of absolute good and bad, we choose to approach reality circumstantially, asking concretely what needs to be done in this moment. To be sure, we take into account the likely effects of our actions on others and on ourselves. But philosophical speculation about ideals too easily becomes a distraction from engaging in what needs doing right now.

WORKING WITHIN THE FLUX

In constructive living we emphasize the changeableness of feelings. A parallel Buddhist principle is *mujo,* "all is flux." Everything is always changing. Perhaps so, yet even the Zen monk in training finds that doing what needs to be done provides some stability and order and purposeful direction in this ever-changing world. The monk may find that what needs to be done is sitting meditation, sweeping, mopping, chanting, eating in a particular fashion, and so forth.

We, too, create some stability, order, and direction through purposeful behavior. Despite the flux of feelings and head-tripping we can reach the haven of disciplined behavior. We have come full circle to the beginning passage on the equivalence of means and ends. The order and stability exist as we create them by our doing. As you read these words, you are already changed. That is, the quality of your attentive reading is already important change, whatever the value of the content of this essay. What you are doing now isn't "preparing" you for self-improvement. It either *is* self-improvement or it is not. The quality of the doing is vital.

Television and Telling Tales

On a January 1985 episode of "St. Elsewhere" I heard, "You're not a failure until you quit trying" and "I love you but you've got to finish what you start."

Terrific! Such advice is more sound than the stale go-with-your-feelings suggestions seen so often in the media.

About the same time I was flipping back and forth between two television programs—one highlighting the Miss Teen USA Pageant and the other documenting gang violence in Los Angeles. The innocent smiles and "go for it" hopefulness were juxtaposed with the firebombed houses and cigarette-burned bodies.

It is tempting to think that only the latter is actual or honest, that the sweet smiles hide ignorance of the "real world." But such is not the case. There are both sorts of realities in this world, and many more, besides. There is truth in both programs, truth worth learning. Our reality may bring us mostly one sort or mostly the other or neither or both. We must not close our eyes to what reality presents to us. And we need not think that someone else's reality is more real than our own.

One of the changes that seems to have resulted, in part, from television viewing is that many people have ceased to consider others' stories worth listening to. Unless a person is beautiful or handsome or powerful or worthy of sponsors and commercials, he finds it more and more difficult to get an audience. In pretelevision America we used to sit with family and guests and strangers swapping tales from our life stories. We took the time to find out what was interesting about Uncle Fritz and Grandma Copeland. We learned which of their stories from which part of their lives was most likely to prove amusing or instructive. By listening to what they had to say, we learned that they were much like us. And we learned how we were different the same way.

Try to get young people to sit still to converse with adult guests these days. The kids are off to watch television as fast as propriety and parents permit. It is sad. There are more dimensions to Aunt Margaret than to "Magnum." There is a depth of character that comes because Aunt Margaret actually lived years in those places and actually had those experiences she talks about (at least most of them). She wasn't created by a bright writer or two for an existence that continues for thirty or sixty minutes each week until viewers get tired of watching her. Aunt Margaret has lots to teach us—if we take the time to listen.

The work of counseling for constructive living is a privileged pursuit. One benefit is that we are permitted to listen to stories of Aunt Margarets and Uncle Herberts. They want and need to tell someone what has been going on in their lives. They need to spell out the intricately winding roads of misery they face, what they have tried for shortcuts and detours, how tired they are having come so long a life journey.

We don't emphasize the past in Morita guidance. We don't try to find some point in time where someone strayed onto the wrong track or was forced off the main road by someone else. When I was asked recently by a student, "Where did I go wrong?" I was quick to point out that there are countless choices made and still to be made in his life. We must keep making them, and we make them with as much sensitivity and sanity as lies in us. Although we don't dwell on past mistakes or successes, my students still may need to talk about such things to clear the air. Such a process is still a lot of effort away from constructive living, but it may be necessary along the way.

I find no difficulty in allowing those stories during some of our counseling sessions. We won't devote all our time to them, but they are worth telling and worth hearing. I suspect that if there were less television watching in our world, there would be less need for the ears of the constructive living guide.

The students may have strong needs to tell their stories, but they need to listen, too. One of the exercises we suggest to our students is to look up someone they normally avoid, engage him or her in conversation, and uncover some interesting side of that person. There is a tale in that person that is deserving of our ears and our time. It may take skill to uncover the story. Such an exercise is also valuable for learning the techniques of interviewing, or of simply listening well. A skill like that can give television sets a lot of time off.

Scenes

When my clients talk about the events of the past week, they tend to talk in terms of scenes or episodes. These scenes have clear beginnings and endings. I find myself listening to a brief tale organized like a television story. I believe that my clients have been influenced by television and other media to carve up their experience into scenes. I often need to ask, "What did you do next?" I want to know what my student did after what he or she thought was the end of the scene.

Let me offer an example. Clyde tells me of the scene in which he embarrassed himself before his fellow cooking-school classmates by raising his hand, then forgetting what he wanted to ask. He finishes by telling me he felt like crawling into a hole to escape their eyes. As far as Clyde was concerned, the scene ended there.

"What did you do next?" I ask.

"What do you mean?"

"I want to know what you did right after that, while you were feeling embarrassed."

"Well, the teacher went on with his lecture, so I grabbed my pen and started taking notes again."

Clyde had come a long way from the days in which embarrassment was followed by hours of self-recrimination and even absences from school. If he had chosen to end his "scene" a bit later, he would have turned out to be a hero instead of a goat. The forgetting was not controllable directly by his will. With his best effort he couldn't come up with the question that caused him to raise his hand. But what he did while feeling embarrassed was another opportunity for success (in this case, taking notes). And Clyde succeeded.

Life doesn't present itself in episodes or scenes. It is a continuous flow of opportunities, failures, successes, punctuated only by periods of sleep—and sometimes then, too, we experience the flow of dreams. When failure looms (or when success lies within reach), the important question to be asking continues to be, "What has reality brought that needs to be done?" Then, what did you do next?

Why Water Bears No Scars

To some degree we all write the novels of our lives in our minds. We organize our pasts to give ourselves orderly and memorable histories (there are entire psychotherapy systems devoted to that task); we create dramas and villains and elaborate plots. We anticipate new chapters and a variety of endings. And, above all, we create in our minds the character we will play in our life novels.

Life does not come to us in the form of a novel. It doesn't bring the orderliness and consistency of a structured creation. Our minds reorganize experience to fit the scripted form we create for ourselves. That is why we may scar ourselves unnecessarily. We can build in unnecessary pain in our lives by creating tragedies when there are only events, by creating consistently weak and suffering characters when there are only moments and more moments of life experience.

This book is about the organizing screen our minds throw up to create life novels. It is about learning to connect more closely with the infinitely more interesting and varied reality that presents itself to us. It is about abandoning the dependence on scripting our lives for suffering and about getting on with living them constructively, productively. The distorted order created by saying, "I am this sort of person," "My past was flawed in such and such a way," "She shouldn't be the way she is," "I'll never become that sort of person," "Life will always bring me these kinds of prob-

DAVID K. REYNOLDS

lems," "There is no future for someone like me," is a fictitious organization of reality created by the mind. In this book we'll consider ways and offer exercises that help us to view reality on a more basic and more flexible level. This realistic perspective will go a long way toward allowing us to make needed moment-by-moment changes in our lives.

Can you already see that life never presents us with "problems," only with events? Can you already see that the notion of "personality" is a sort of abstracted fiction that doesn't exist in our everyday lives? Can you already see that our memories of the past and our explanations of why we did what we did in the past are oversimplified caricatures of what we were really experiencing then? Can you already see that the changeableness that is you need not be bound by labels such as "neurotic" or "lazy" or "coldhearted" or "lonely" or "insecure"? If you already see and live these truths, then there is really no need to read further. You already possess the freedom offered here. You are already freed from your life novel. You are living in reality.

Tokuko Shimbo is the wife of a well-known Morita therapist in Tokyo. She has come to know the principles of constructive living intimately. She considers the neurotic people she encounters to be "tone deaf about life *(seikatsu onchi)*." They try to force the natural pitch and rhythm of everyday life into an artificially constructed image of how life ought to be scripted. They force their life-novel scripts on others. They miss the melody of what is.

A rushing stream of water flows around the obstacles that stand in its way. It doesn't stop to dwell on the injuries sustained by a projecting rock or a submerged log. It keeps moving toward its goal, encountering each difficulty as it appears, responding actively, then moving along downstream. The stream has no imagination to create unchanging stories of its existence. It washes away its own wounds in its present purposefulness. The water bears no scars.

Water Holds Great Power

It seems to me that Western psychotherapies play on the weakness of patients. The goals of Western therapies involve easing the lives of the patients, reducing their anxiety, supporting them. Western therapies are soft and sympathetic; the therapists tend to side with their clients against others who are seen as the cause of their clients' troubles.

On the surface, therapies with their roots in Japanese wisdom appear to be severe, even uncaring toward clients' suffering. Not only do they take the clients' suffering for granted, they may assign difficult tasks that actually cause more misery (temporarily). What underlies such practices is the recognition of the client's true strength of character. Easing the client's way won't help him or her find true depth of character. Easing life circumstances won't allow the client to develop the confidence that comes with over-coming those circumstances.

It isn't that I don't care about my students' pain. It is just that trying to erase it will only cause more pain in the long run. Learning to act on life in a constructive manner while hurting puts the pain into perspective. The student learns that the dimension of hurt-no-hurt isn't the only one or even the major one along which life can be lived. The satisfaction of giving to someone else while one is suffering, without mentioning a word about one's own plight, deepens character. That lesson cannot be learned while

DAVID K. REYNOLDS

one is complaining to all who will listen about one's personal dilemmas.

My American client may misunderstand these words. I am not recommending denial or suppression of one's own pain in favor of serving others. Pain has a way of reminding us of its existence over and over again, anyway. Isn't that your experience? But as the misery (or shyness or obsession or fear or grief or feeling of failure or any other emotion) surfaces and we notice it, we need not let that misery prescribe our actions. We need not let it dominate us. Our choice in the area of behavior remains.

Development of character (as opposed to relief from suffering) seems to have been more emphasized at other times in Western history than it is now. Take Rudyard Kipling's famous poem "If," for example:

If you can keep your head when all about you
Are losing theirs and blaming it on you,
If you can trust yourself when all men doubt you
But make allowance for their doubting, too;
If you can wait and not be tired of waiting
Or being lied about, don't deal in lies,
Or being hated, don't give way to hating,
And yet don't look too good, nor talk too wise.

If you can dream—and not make dreams your master.
If you can think—and not make thoughts your aim,
If you can meet with Triumph and Disaster,
And treat those two imposters just the same;
If you can bear to hear the truth you've spoken
Twisted by knaves to make a trap for fools,
Or watch the things you gave your life to broken,
And stoop to build 'em up with worn out tools.

If you can make one heap of all your winnings
And risk it on one turn of pitch-and-toss,
And lose, and start again at your beginnings
And never breathe a word about your loss;

If you can force your heart and nerve and sinew
To serve your turn long after they are gone,
And so hold on when there is nothing in you
Except the Will which says to them "Hold on!"

If you can talk with crowds and keep your virtue,
Or walk with Kings—nor lose the common touch,
If neither foes nor loving friends can hurt you,
And all men count with you, but none too much;
If you can fill the unforgiving minute,
With sixty seconds worth of distance run,
Yours is the earth and everything that's in it,
And—which is more—you'll be a Man, my son!

For the most part, Kipling was writing about behavior, about doing. Nearly all of this poem offers direct application for those who want to try a constructive approach to life. It suggests a path toward building character.

From our point of view, however, there are a few pieces of advice in "If" that must be interpreted carefully to avoid possible pitfalls.

"If you can trust yourself when all men doubt you" might lead some perfectionistic people to try to create self-trust, somehow, thinking it is necessary for effective living. Trust is a sort of feeling or attitude. It isn't controllable directly by the will. Without confidence, without self-trust, it is possible to do what needs doing in life while making allowances for the doubts of others. Trusting ourselves usually comes after we have created a history of successful, trustworthy activities. Self-trust isn't necessary for getting started.

It's all right to be "tired of waiting." The important thing is to wait, tired or not, when waiting is what needs to be done. And it's all right to "give way to hating," provided that the hating isn't allowed to explode into destructive behavior. To be sure, life is easier and more pleasant when we feel patience and when we are free from hate, when our feelings and our behaviors flow smoothly in parallel channels. Unfortunately, I know of no one for whom that ideal mesh of feelings and behavior persists without interruption. Keeping behavior under responsible control is a realistic goal that takes much effort and attention. Then feelings will take care of themselves.

Along the same lines I suspect that Kipling wasn't recommending insensitivity toward foes and friends when he wrote "If neither foes nor loving friends can hurt you." We do feel hurt by friends and foes, at times. To feel that hurt is a natural human capacity. Rather than trying to become someone who doesn't feel the pain, it is more realistic and finer to become one who doesn't let the hurt dictate what one does. The hurt can be recognized and accepted while the doing of this moment's deeds proceeds in a positive direction.

In sum, the wisdom in Kipling's "If" offers constructive advice for daily living. Translating it into this moment's action requires careful thought and much practice. Kipling doesn't write about complete self-understanding; he writes about sculpting a solid character, about building a life.

Washing Away Our Scars

Stephen wakes up in the morning feeling like a failure. He wishes the feeling would go away. But Stephen is not living a life that anyone would call successful. The message his mind is sending him seems perfectly appropriate and even positive. That is, his mind is telling him (and me) that it won't be satisfied with the passive, nonconstructive life Stephen is leading. Oddly, I am encouraged by this discomforting communication.

Rather than trying to erase this important message with positive thinking or tranquilizers, I recommend to Stephen that he thank his mind each time that message of dissatisfaction appears. His mind will continue to make him miserable until he changes his actions. After expressing gratitude for the message, he needs to turn immediately to what needs doing right now that will change his failing lifestyle.

At a recent meeting of the Hakkenkai Moritist organization in Japan a young woman asked my advice about her problem with needles and pins. She worries that she has lost a needle somewhere. Even when she counts the needles before and after using them and she comes up with the same number, she worries that she lost one on an earlier occasion.

I told her that being careful about needles is not her problem. It is a good idea to be careful about them. People who are careless in such matters are likely to find themselves painfully reminded of

DAVID K. REYNOLDS

their negligence. Her problem is in not doing the next thing that needs to be done after checking that she has properly returned all the needles and pins she used during a sewing session.

When she develops the habit of turning to the next task immediately and smoothly, her attention will be drawn into the work or play at hand and won't linger on the past matter of the needles. Although she believes that her difficulty lies in her fixation on the needles, it really lies within the later matter of what she does (or doesn't do). The concern about needles—like the worry before an examination or the anxiety about one's health or the dread of learning to drive or the fear of making a mistake in front of others or the shyness when making a new acquaintance—is natural. Anxiety is natural. Shyness is natural. Anticipatory worry is natural. All feelings are natural. They are only problems when we allow them to hinder what we do. They become problems when we try to struggle with them and try to control them with our will.

A much better strategy—the one I suggested to this young lady—is to accept the concern as it is, as part of her reality at the moment, and get on about the cooking or vacuuming or laundering or dressing for the party or whatever.

Helen tells me her parents don't properly love her. I ask her to look at the specific ways in which her failure to hold down a job, her shyness, and her reluctance to talk to her parents have caused trouble for them. Stacy notes that his wife and children blame him for being either too confining or too lax in the way he disciplines his children. His children show adolescent rebelliousness, and his wife is not the perfect housekeeper he wishes her to be. I ask him to attend to the favors these household members bestow on him and to offer a word of gratitude for even the smallest thoughtful deed. Stacy tells me that he already reminds his daughter when she fails to say thank you at an appropriate time. I point out that it is *his* words of thanks that are at issue here, not his daughter's. He is having no trouble with such matters, he insists. I ask him to go even beyond the level he has achieved so far, to offer verbal appreciation for the slightest effort of his wife and children, no matter whether he truly feels the circumstance to be trivial, no matter whether he sees zero positive response from them to his efforts, no matter whether he is feeling angry or regretful or unappreciated at the time. The form alone is sufficient at this stage of study.

People who suffer a great deal from anxiety may not recognize the inconvenience their problems are causing others around them. Although some of my students are acutely aware of difficulties they cause others (and that awareness adds to their misery), neither those who are aware nor those who are unaware are actively involved in reducing the inconvenience of others. They are so involved in fighting their own condition that they lack energy and attention to be helpful to others.

Often, I find it useful to recommend that my students reflect on the specific, concrete ways in which their neurotic behavior causes trouble to people around them. At the same time I ask them to pay attention to the efforts of others in their behalf. There is immediate resistance whenever these combined exercises are assigned. Who wants to work on an assignment that will make them feel guilty? What have others ever done for them? Why not work directly on their own personal problem rather than paying so much attention to others? The resistance to these assignments takes many forms—some complain, some forget to carry them out, some forget what the assignment was, some don't return for another session, some simply refuse to consider such a foolish task. But those who diligently look at the troubles they cause others and the favors others are doing for them find the exercise of great value.

Letters

LETTERS OF GRATITUDE

Some of my students still cling to old ways of being in old relationships. Young adults who have learned in other therapies all the ways their parents have twisted their characters often fall into this category. So do women who have broken off with someone they lived with for years. These students are still tied to the old relationships even though they may have separated from them for years.

One of the assignments I offer these students is to write a letter expressing gratitude for specific deeds of kindness the other person showed them in the past. For example, the letter might contain thanks for the night a parent went out in a downpour to get cough medicine for the student's whooping cough. Or it might include words of thanks for the former spouse's taking a day off from work to comfort the student when she was depressed. For specific gifts, specific acts, specific words; on specific dates at specific places whenever possible. And the letter is to contain no mention of what the student did for the other person or what the other person did to cause trouble or misery to the student. It is strictly a letter of gratitude.

Needless to say, there is much resistance to writing such a

letter. The resistance takes many forms. The student may fear that such a letter would be interpreted as an admission of the student's failure and blame in the relationship. The student may worry that such a letter will be taken as an overture to rekindle a close relationship. The student is quite likely to hold that the recipient of such a letter wouldn't deserve it. The anger and hurt are still strong enough to make writing such a letter difficult.

The resistance to the assignment helps the student to see the depth of the feelings still attached to the relationship. What the student may have thought was safely put behind still exerts a drag on what is being done now. There is no possibility of reestablishing a different kind of relationship (be it as fellow adults or distant strangers or friends) as long as this baggage from the past hampers current movement. The student wants to maintain a memory image of the other as hurtful and ungiving. What has happened is that a certain amount of the student's energy has been diverted to suppressing memories of the acts of the other person's kindness. This assignment forces the student to recall past events in a more balanced fashion. The memories of pain will not disappear. But they come to coexist alongside the memories of services and gifts and, perhaps, of the student's own contribution to the other person's frustration and misery.

When the letter is at last written, there is another moment of truth. To make the irrevocable step of sending it may be frightening. The student must truly understand the principle that everyone is responsible for his or her own behavior. We cannot control how anyone else will respond to what we do. Yet we must continue to hold ourselves responsible for what we do, for our response to the reactions of others. The letter may be used against us, it may be misinterpreted, it may be disregarded, ignored. We build our evaluation of the letter on the rightness of our writing it, not on the response of the recipient. To be tied to evaluating the letter in terms of the other's response is still to be tied to the relationship. To write and send such a letter regardless of what that response might be is to be free.

These letters may be the most difficult to write. But often they are necessary for real progress in character development to occur. When written, they are evidence that character growth has already taken place.

When there is trouble between people, some fault lies on both sides. We prefer to look at the causes that lie in others rather than examining our own contributions to the discord. Writing a letter of apology brings up issues of image and pride. How will the reader take what I have written? Will the letter be used against me in the future? Will the letter be proof of my opponent's victory and my defeat?

A properly written letter of apology contains no hint of the recipient's contribution to the problem. It contains detailed accounts of the writer's errors, specific apologies, and offers to make restitution when appropriate. The tone is not resigned or humorous or satirical. We know the devious means by which we carry out an assignment while avoiding the spirit of the task.

This type of letter is not written for masochistic delight. We carry with us tasks that are unfinished. Unfinished business in old relationships can affect current ones. Ongoing relationships need to be "cleaned up" periodically. These letters tell someone that they were worth our time, our effort, our apology. They are.

CORRESPONDENCE GUIDANCE

Some students of this constructive lifestyle find it difficult or impossible to come to weekly individual or group sessions. They may live in an area that has no teacher/guide yet. Reading the literature and practicing the assignments on their own provides some help, but they have specific questions and desire a more personal, individualized course for self-growth. These students may undertake training through correspondence.

Morita therapists in Japan have offered correspondence counseling (*tegami sodan*, in Japanese) for many years. We have begun offering the same service in the West for nearly ten years now.

A typical response during a course of guidance by mail follows. It has been edited to protect the identity of the correspondent. He was an office manager in his late twenties with an introspective and philosophical bent. Much of his suffering and most of his questions centered around existential concerns and problems with his fiancée, Karen.

Dear X:

Thank you for the information and the check. You did a careful and diligent job on the time-sampled schedule; your questions are thoughtful; your writing is legible—you are a serious student. First, some logistics. I'll be in Japan March 31–June 19. My address there is:

David K. Reynolds, Ph.D.
c/o Dr. Shimbo
1-8-2-701 Gohongi
Meguro-ku, Tokyo 153
Japan (Phone:[Tokyo] 719-4555)

Please make sure you copy each letter you send me so that you can refer back to it when reading my comments. Some of the assignments will have purposes that you readily understand; some will have purposes that are written in the books but have additional purposes that aren't written in them; in others you'll have to figure out the purposes while doing them. Just give them a try and see what happens. If you doubt the usefulness for you, that's fine; it's up to you to do them or not. But I believe that you will find that the assignments are useful, whatever doubts you may entertain initially.

Let's begin with some initial responses to your questions:

Paying full attention is what you were doing when you wrote the question in the letter.

What is your purpose in sitting meditation? In other words, what is the goal? If there is something you have decided is more important than sitting each morning, then do it. If not, sit "well," without wishing you were elsewhere, without getting away from it early on a whim. When something more important appears, then leave the sitting immediately without leaving your mind back in the sitting.

Purposeful living means being able to answer the question "Why am I doing this now?" at any moment. It is the opposite of aimless moments. In another sense it is the opposite of feeling-centeredness. The focus is on doing/action/behavior that is goal-directed while feelings are noted (not supressed or ignored) and used as information. The behavior is goal-pulled rather than feeling-pushed.

About Christianity and constructive living: I find no difference between "God's Will for my life" and "What reality presents that needs doing." That is, God's Will for me is the reality presented to me. Christian principles of prayer, tithing, worshiping in groups, and so on all have a practical aspect understood in terms of what we *do* (regardless of whether we feel angry, devoted, or guilty in regard to the Church at any moment), can provide stability and order in our lives, and change who we are. There's no necessity to make the connection as I do; we can discuss details more if you have specific questions. Better to become skillful at constructive living first.

"Acceptance" means recognizing what is. Wishing it were otherwise changes nothing. When we have a clear sense of how things are, we are in the best position to do our best to change them for the better. But when we do everything we can and the changes we want don't appear, that reality we must accept, too. And, perhaps, work some more. Watch and see how much of your anger problem is connected with your lack of acceptance of how things are and your inability to control reality directly, immediately the way you would like. Our training won't make the anger go away. But you'll get good at accepting the anger, too, without acting from it; and then the anger will begin to become less obtrusive. Fatalism is far from acceptance.

"Principles" are some of the criteria by which we decide what needs to be done. Principles help focus on our purposes.

There's no problem with being hypocritical if your purpose is blameless. When I'm upset and still present a calm facade to a sobbing student, then I'm willing to be called hypocritical. I would prefer to use the term to describe someone who conceals evil actions with a face of saintliness (we all fit that definition at times). To accept unpleasant feelings and stay in control of behavior isn't hypocritical in this sense; it is noble. Feelings are neither good nor bad, just natural phenomena—like the breeze. It is the doing that can be seen in terms of good and bad meaningfully.

Acting and writing are not escapes from reality, as you know. They are ways we create reality in certain moments. We do them with full attention. I read science fiction some and I like Walker Percy, the novelist. Sometimes reading needs to be done. The problem appears when people read novels in order to avoid doing something that needs doing. Be careful of your tendency to try to apply some sort of across-the-board evaluation good/bad and so forth. That Catholic background . . . Just do what you *know* you need to be about in this very moment and these philosophical questions will seem less important to you. Work on the doing, the rest will become clear.

Assignments: Please begin a journal of the sort described in Exercise III, page 84, of *Constructive Living*. Send me any week's entries, one page per day, in your next letter.

Please begin considering Koan 3, page 23, in *Playing Ball or Running Water*. Consider various responses. Critique each one until you find one that is blameless, perfect. Send me a summary of what occurred to you and the critiques.

Thank Karen ten times each day (whether you feel grateful or not). Thank objects (your car, pen, whatever) ten times a day (aloud is preferable, but in private is all right). Write about the exercise.

Ask questions, let me know what is going on in your life. Keep up the practice, observing the waxing and waning of interest and enthusiasm. Write again when that needs to be done. Send check as before; I'll reply from wherever I am at the time. Hold to your purpose,

David K. Reynolds

Realism

Anyone who has spent years working in a garden or in the fields knows impermanence intimately. We see the cycle of seasons, the coming and going of insects, droughts, freezes, rot, the seeds that sprout or die, the life cycles of plants, the bountiful harvests and the lean. It is all change. There is nothing that can be counted on with certainty to be exactly as it was last year. Our only recourse is to keep on fitting what we do, adapting who we are, to the constantly changing circumstances.

It does no good to tell the grasshopper eating the soybean leaves, "You really shouldn't be doing that." Wishing the rain would stop (or come) doesn't affect the weather or the plants. Analyzing how we feel about fungus doesn't save the cabbage. We need a more realistic perspective and straightforward action to have a chance to effect the changes we desire.

I am not being passive or resigned when I emphasize the changeableness of the world and the necessity of our adapting to it. Only when we have a clear vision of this flux and our place in it does our effort mean something. To work and succeed and play and love while pretending it will all last, while ignoring the fragile "momentariness" of it all, is to miss the chance for depth in all these activities. To try *while dying*, to love *while changing*, to play *while acknowledging the impermanence* allows a kind of nobility to the simplest act, to something that was only childish escape before.

There is nothing ennobling about suffering itself. But in *striving while suffering* we move beyond ourselves to become new creatures—whether the striving attains what we set out to accomplish or not. Pain and self-doubt and fear and anger don't necessarily stimulate growth, but they do permit it. When the effort is there. Change is inevitable. In the garden, in us. Some of the change we can influence, some we cannot. Our fundamental hope lies in affecting the change that *is* us.

Recent Examples

Fred tells me that the work he put in yesterday on his accounts was "totally wasted." His life is "absolutely awful." He is a "complete failure," "worthless," "suppressed by everything and everybody." Immediately and automatically Fred attaches a strong value label to thoughts as they arise in his mind. This habit of thinking is a combination of the neurotic "all or nothing" attitude and neurotic perfectionism that Morita therapists have written about for years.

A cornerstone of constructive living is the attitude of *arugamama*. Arugamama is precisely the opposite attitude to that of Fred's. Arugamama means accepting reality as it is—it means literally, "as it is." As reality presents itself to our senses, our minds organize the stimuli into meaningful patterns. Some people have developed the mental habit of attaching extreme value labels and absolutist adjectives to these patterned events. When it is hot, it is "terribly" hot; when it is cold, it is "unbearably" cold. The red light that halts their progress is a "damned" red light. The malfunctioning can opener "never" works right. And so on.

These poor habits of thought interfere with the readiness of the neurotic person to respond promptly and properly to the needs of the situation. Obstacles appear insurmountable, setbacks seem devastating, inconveniences become paralyzing. The first step in changing this unsatisfying orientation is to notice that it occurs. I frequently interrupt Fred's long, complaining monologues to point out his use of absolutes and strong value labels in his speech. Fred is a quick-minded fellow. He begins to notice them and point them out himself with a small smile of recognition. He begins joining the game of identification.

Habits take time to break, just as they took time to form. So Fred will fall back into neurotic thought patterns again and again before breaking through them. One of the techniques that will help Fred is to present him with new stimuli he hasn't already labeled and dismissed. Fred is self-employed. His business allows him to leave his office and warehouse when he wants, but in fact he stays there, practically lives there, nearly all of his waking hours. I assign long walks, trips to the beach and to local parks, visits to nearby university research libraries. These novel inputs from reality will present Fred with the opportunity to develop the new habits of thinking that we talk about in our therapy sessions.

Much of my work consists of saying the same things over and over again in novel ways so as to hold the attention of my clients. Moritist theory is not so complex. It is the detailed application of the theory that takes minute attention and persistence. By using a variety of illustrations and analogies I can hold the client's attention and reinforce the points of constructive living through repetition. Novelty and surprise are useful tools in getting my job done.

Sal is in his late thirties and not doing much with his life, according to his mother's point of view. She has big plans for Sal. She wants him to go to a university for advanced degrees in engineering. She wants him to wear a white shirt and tie and to work in an office. Sal, on the other hand, enjoys working with his hands. He is a skillful mechanic, in need of the physical activity and concrete problem solving that working on an automobile can provide.

Sal isn't stupid. He realizes that he must do what he knows needs to be done, not what his mother has decided for him. He sometimes argues with her over the issue of his career. Sal tries to convince her that she should see things his way; after all, it is his life and his work they are talking about. Sal's mistake is in trying to make his mother satisfied with his choice of occupations. Her opinions are fine just as they are.

Sal is trying to accomplish precisely what he objects to in his mother's efforts. He is trying to impose his choice and will upon her. There is no need for them to view this issue with the same eyes. Allowing his mother her own perspective could even provide her with a model for her eventual allowance of Sal's perspective. Confrontation is worse than useless in this situation; it is actually harmful. Acceptance and waiting are more likely to resolve the difficulty. Meanwhile, Sal must go steadily about his chosen work—doing it with attention and craftsmanship—without trying to control the uncontrollable.

When Morita was treating a woman with dirt phobia, he took her toothbrush from her after she had used it and, without washing it, brushed his own teeth with it. The patient was shocked to see this highly respected professor of psychiatry using her "contaminated" toothbrush. The impression had such impact that her symptoms were relieved. Morita had demonstrated again the importance of action as a teaching device. Verbal instruction and probing insight may be helpful in the resolution of neurotic problems, but they aren't sufficient in themselves, either for the therapist or for the client.

Throughout Morita therapy there are parallels between the therapist's action and attitude and that which is expected from the clients in order to surmount their disorders. Therapists actually model the lifeway they are recommending to their clients.

It is 7:30 A.M. I just finished talking with a client for a half an hour on the telephone. Paul called to tell me about how terrible his life is these days. An attorney failed to file some court papers resulting in the loss of thousands of dollars. A worker who was hired to repair some of Paul's property in preparation for selling it doesn't appear to be doing any work, and Paul is having difficulty contacting the man. After working on a number of drafts of a business letter Paul finally called a friend to write it for him. On and on, Paul complains about the poor service he is getting from reality.

I assigned Paul the task of speaking only positively for the rest of the day. We are scheduled for an individual therapy session tomorrow morning. Until that time Paul is to refrain from complaining to anyone about anything. He is to find something positive to say to everyone he encounters. He is to express praise and gratitude to all who come in contact with him today regardless of how he really feels. I instructed him to be an actor, to play a part until the part becomes his reality.

I am instructing Paul to bottle up his dissatisfaction rather than expressing it. I am instructing him to be "unreal" in the sense of acting along lines that aren't in accord with his feelings. My guidance would bring about shocked horror in some therapy circles. But for Paul in this time and in these circumstances such an assignment is appropriate. And Paul himself knows it! He has no trouble expressing his unhappiness about the way the world is treating him. He has been expressive in this way for years—and the complaints have led him into deeper and deeper misery. Paul senses that Morita's approach offers a way out of his negativism. In the past when Paul was true to his feelings, he was only acting in concert with some of his feelings, the ones he chose to focus on, the negative ones. There are other feelings in Paul that have been ignored and underplayed. Those feelings accompany desires to grow and give to others and stretch out his life in a more positive direction. We shall see how much effort he puts into practicing the assignments. Because it is the doing that will change Paul's feelings and not vice versa.

PART II

MORITA'S SAYINGS

wwwww
wwwww
wwwww

Constructive Living Principles

Morita wrote and said much that is worth quoting. Shigehisa Aoki (1976), for example, collected a scattering of Morita's observations and wisdom. Yozo Hasegawa (1985) edited another collection, focusing on neurosis and its treatment. The entire set of *Collected Writings of Morita Shoma* fills six volumes in Japanese. I offer here a selection of Morita's insights and observations with expanded and interpreted commentary for modern times.

1. RELY ON REALITY, NOT A PERSON OR A SYSTEM OF THOUGHT.

When a person relies on a Morita guide or on the Morita way to handle life's problems, he or she has not yet (cured) graduated from the course of constructive living. When accepting feelings is natural, when doing what needs doing is the only thing one considers moment by moment, then one has graduated. There is no need to impose a "system" or a "teacher" on the natural process of being natural.

Some students want to identify with a named lifeway or a person rather than just living constructively. I know of one lady who carries around a worn copy of a book on Morita therapy as though it were an amulet. Another carries a photo of her therapist with her when she goes out of the house. Others keep Morita's photo and calligraphy hanging on the walls of their homes and offices. Morita recognized the tendancy of people to reify and deify. His opposition to this tendency was based on the fundamental premise that whatever takes us away from straightforward encounters with reality is harmful.

A named system or person is a convenient way of rallying people who share views and experiences of training and everyday life. Yet there is a freeing step that comes with truly integrating the principles into everyday life without having to see oneself always drawing strength from a therapist or group. But even with independence one isn't freed from the gratitude to Morita or to one's teacher or supporting others. One sees that these others, too, were just doing what needed doing at the time.

2. EVERY PHENOMENON HAS TWO SIDES. FOR EVERYTHING THERE IS BENEFIT AND HARM, GAINING AND LOSING.

Morita wasn't referring here to the old saw that every dispute must have arguments on both sides. He was reflecting, from a Taoist or Zen-like perspective, that everything contains within itself, or implies, the elements of its opposite. We cannot distinguish trouble without knowing relief; we cannot know what failure is without knowing what success is; life has meaning only when juxtaposed with death. Such thinking is well represented in Jungian thought, as well.

One implication is that our suffering implies or carries with it nonsuffering. The persistence that shows itself as obsessing and holding on to ideas and habits and people long after we should let them go also shows itself as diligence in pursuing a course of self-growth, working long and hard on a project, holding to our principles and goals when others drop away. The persistence is neither good nor bad, or it is both, if you prefer. Similarly, a toothache highlights the relief we feel later and draws attention to the contribution of that tooth to our well-being. There is an old Zen saying that when the shoe fits, we forget the foot.

I am not saying here that all misery is good (because it feels so

DAVID K. REYNOLDS

good when it stops). But I am asserting that all misery holds the implication of relief or no-misery. That may sound like small philosophical comfort when we are in the midst of hurting. But to see the hurt as only bad, destructive, limiting is to blind oneself to another side of that hurt. Some of my students aren't hurting enough. They hurt just enough to feel mildly uncomfortable and not enough to use the hurt to push themselves to make basic changes in their lives.

Today goes, tomorrow comes; I lose innocence, I gain experience; the air comes into my lungs, changes, returns, changes; now in need of support, now supporting; now understood, now understanding; now hurt by my sensitivity, now pleased by it. Both sides important, real, true.

3. FOLLOW THE LAWS OF NATURE. BE REALISTIC.

There is no use trying to make death pleasant or life free of anxiety. Death is fearful, though it may provide relief from some of our familiar suffering. Our very bodies struggle and struggle to keep us alive. Yet as we live day by day, life presents us with events that result in pain, worry, doubt, anger, and other unpleasantness. There are natural limits to our life freedom, whatever may be the degree of our political freedom.

This approach to life involves realism in its most primitive sense. We must recognize the boundaries and organization that reality places on our existence. We must study and learn the possibilities and restrictions of the natural world, that is, of reality. And we must abide by them. We dare not ignore them. Genuine freedom can arise only when we recognize the limits placed on us. Again, the previous principle "two sides to every phenomenon" applies. Realizing the limits of reality contains the corresponding recognition of the freedom that reality presents to us.

4. NO GREAT PERSON WAS EVER FREE OF GREAT SUFFERING.

When one looks carefully at the biographies of the truly great humans who left their mark on the history of mankind, one will always find great suffering. Particularly in the teens and twenties many eminent psychological and spiritual leaders experienced valuable lessons as they overcame severe shyness, phobias, obsessions, and/or feelings of inadequacy. Morita himself, Hakuin, the Zen master, Martin Luther, and Freud are typically offered as examples. They went on to apply the principles they learned about pain and possibility throughout their lives. It's not unreasonable to consider that the suffering permitted their greatness.

5. FORGET ABOUT TRYING TO CURE YOURSELF.

It is natural to want to be free of hurt, to want to sleep well every night, to want total confidence in every situation, to want calm self-possession in any emergency. But those who exert effort to achieve these impossible goals disappoint themselves and create even more problems in their lives.

6. IF YOU FEEL NO SHYNESS AROUND THE PERSON YOU LOVE, THEN YOU'RE PROBABLY NOT IN LOVE.

Young people, in particular, suffer from the peculiar idea that they should always be in control of their feelings. They want always to feel relaxed and calm in front of someone they desire to impress. They worry that their shyness will interfere with their making genuine human contact with someone they care about.

But when we really value someone else, we feel a degree of hesitation and shyness toward him or her. Some adults have learned to suppress their awareness of this tendency, but it is there nonetheless. It is natural to want to show our best side to those we love. It is natural to fear the revelation of our faults and weaknesses to these special others. Our shyness comes from the awareness of our own inadequacies and an idealistic evaluation of the one we love.

Part of growing up involves the acceptance of this shyness in ourselves and learning to ask for the telephone number or ask for the date or introduce ourselves or make the phone call in spite of this hesitation. In our neurotic moments we project in our minds what might happen, what he or she might say, what refusal we might face, what embarrassment we would feel if we were to stammer or blush. In social life our task isn't to feel like James Bond or Princess Diana at all times. Rather, we do what is appropriate, wait for reality (in this case, the person we love) to respond, and then act appropriately on the basis of that new information from reality. Such a life strategy is much more feasible than trying to extinguish our shyness or create an attitude of extreme confidence.

There is, in my view, a sort of purity in the shyness that love produces. It is painful, but it is also rather touching and appealing to see. There is no need to try to do away with this very human characteristic. What we must learn to do is to live constructively alongside it. As we do so, the intensity and troublesome nature of shyness will naturally decrease.

7. REALISTIC ACTION IS SELF-DEVELOPMENT.

Some people believe that there are special courses they can take or special teachers they can follow to relieve themselves of their suffering. But the most effective means of preparing oneself for constructive living is to live constructively. The measure of an effective course or a wise guide lies in the pressure it exerts on the student to put into practice a realistic lifeway. Beautiful philosophical talk only prepares the student for more philosophical talk.

Morita wrote that there are some lifeways that will withdraw us from the world. We can sit at home all day reading or reciting prayers, and it won't matter whether the wind is blowing or the rain is falling outside. Other lifeways suggest that we should run out in the wind and rain to accomplish our purposes as though storms didn't exist. Such approaches seem rather extreme and unnatural. The first approach requires too much limitation of our action. Moreover, it teaches that our natural feelings of joy and pleasure should be suppressed if we wish to conquer our sorrow and pain. The second approach asks of us the impossible—to ignore the cold, to find hurt pleasurable.

Our strategy of constructive living accepts the reality of hunger when we haven't eaten, cold when we are wet to the skin, joy when we are kissed, and satisfaction when a difficult hurdle is overcome. The feelings are real, the storms outside are real. *And we go about doing what needs doing*, preferring indoor tasks when the rain is falling and outdoor tasks when the sun is shining, running out in the rain only when necessary.

8. NEUROTICALLY SENSITIVE (SHINKEISHITSU) PEOPLE GET CAUGHT UP IN THEORY AND GO TO EXTREMES.

Because shinkeishitsu people lack breadth of experience, they also lack commonsense standards by which to judge their actions. So when they hear of a new faddish cure or when they are advised to try something, they go overboard. I mentioned to one student that some food allergies seem to have strong psychosomatic components, that the symptoms can be influenced by hypnosis. He came back the next week rather ill because he had ignored his previous dietary restrictions and gorged himself on foods that hadn't agreed with him in the past.

We must be careful in guiding overly sensitive clients, who sometimes focus on ideas in a narrow way and pursue them with extreme enthusiasm. We suggest to some students that they study their neurosis, that they observe it objectively. But "study" may be taken to mean reading books about neurosis, and the student may spend day after day immersed in technical texts. Similarly, shinkeishitsu people may move from the extreme of being very sensitive to others' views and opinions to extreme selfishness and insensitivity as they begin to grasp the principles of clinging to one's purpose and doing what needs doing.

9. DON'T WORK IN THE HOPE OF BECOMING CURED. WHEN YOU DRAW A BOW, YOU DON'T HOLD TWO ARROWS.

Some people follow the suggested exercises and assignments in the hope that their neurotic tendencies will disappear. Whatever they discover that needs doing, they do with an eye toward its effect on their developing character. They make the whole process more difficult for themselves because they are constantly checking on their progress.

DAVID K. REYNOLDS

The doing itself is sufficient. The realistic looking at the real world and constructive action on it—that combination is adequate, is growth in itself. Those who "practice" in order to develop joyful satisfaction in doing every task are trying to hold two arrows as they draw their bow. I find no joy in scrubbing my toilet. Scrubbing a toilet need not produce joyful satisfaction. It is enough that the toilet gets clean.

10. I'M ONLY WHAT I AM.

What pressures people put upon themselves! They get sidetracked from the simple goals of doing small services for others into complex goals of trying to appear strong when they feel weak, trying to demonstrate a model of perfection even when they are imperfect, trying to avoid being thought illmannered and worthy of blame despite their common human failings. We sometimes see suffering people making efforts to put on a front so as not to upset their families and friends.

The path to being loved and well-thought-of lies not through some glossy suburb of perfection but along the natural stream of small deeds offered to others. There's no need to try to psyche ourselves into believing how terrific we are. The reality is that we're not terrific all the time. But those rocks and boulders of imperfection need not dam up the stream of thoughtful actions in behalf of others.

11. CURE FOR NEUROSIS LIES NOT IN SUBTRACTING SYMPTOMS BUT IN ADDING CHARACTER.

For some kinds of neurotic suffering we may diligently suppress one sort of problem (obsessing about whether an envelope is properly addressed and stamped before making the irreversible step of placing it in the mail collection box, for example) only to find another emerging (obsessing about sudden death by a heart attack). Freudian psychology offered the world the insight that such symptom substitution occurs because the basic underlying problem hasn't been adequately resolved. Sometimes that underlying problem seems to be a lack of insight into the past and one's strategies for handling memories of the past.

But more often these days the problem lies in an ongoing destructive lifeway, a lack of character and understanding about how to live effectively now, whatever difficulties may have existed in the past. "Cure," a medical term that would be better replaced by "correction of the problem" or "reeducation," is accomplished by building character through proper understanding and purposeful action. Subtracting immediate suffering offers no guarantee that new forms of unnecessary suffering won't emerge. Building a new personality, new character, through constructive living provides a lifelong strategy for handling any suffering when it emerges in any form.

There is no assurance that suffering will disappear from one's life—no one can make such an assurance honestly—but the suffering that comes won't slam on the brakes and send us into the skids as it did before. That's the very best achievement available, as far as I can see.

12. PEOPLE WHO HAVE CONQUERED THEIR NEUROTIC TENDENCIES NATURALLY WANT TO HELP THOSE WHO HAVEN'T DONE SO YET.

As our students progress, we can observe the natural upwelling of the desire to listen with full attention, to offer constructive suggestions, to be helpful in any way possible to those around them who are hurting unnecessarily. Again, such selfless desire is not a result of character development so much as it is a reflection or indication of it. In other words, one doesn't develop one's character and then act to help others. The action *is* the character development.

In the depths of neurotic existence there is no energy or attention for genuine consideration of others' problems. But as the self-centeredness clears, students begin to notice the agony of others. They identify with it, seeing the similarity with their own former state. And they know a way to escape it. They have walked, are walking, away from avoidable misery. Some desire to join groups, write about their experiences, counsel others, and otherwise begin to try to return to the world something of what they have received.

I am not writing here of any religious zeal. There is, ordinarily, no fervor to "spread the word." That fervor, too, would be obsessed with the end result in a way that constructive living is not. Instead, there is just the ongoing concern to do well whatever comes up that needs doing. And the definition of "what needs doing" naturally broadens to include doing what one can for one's fellows.

13. ACTIVITY ALONE ISN'T ENOUGH; THE ACTIVITY MUST FIT THE CIRCUMSTANCES.

Some people seem to think that because sitting around a lot caused them to feel more depressed and isolated, then constant activity will lead to joy and feelings of connection with the world. Without doubt, the human body requires a certain amount of physical activity to maintain its functioning. But the mind isn't satisfied with activity for activity's sake alone. Furthermore, activity for the sake of escape and distraction from neurotic symptoms provides, at best, only temporary relief.

In our approach to enriched living, the goal is to fit our activity to the circumstances we encounter. As always, I must remind the reader that the term "fit" doesn't imply any passive accommodation to circumstances. Sometimes our surroundings require of us active opposition. But always our actions must take careful account of what reality presents to us in the moment. Scattered, unfocused activity is as unhealthy as inactivity.

The values underlying our life strategy include a recognition of the "naturalness" of any circumstance and any feeling state and an underlying goal of maintaining respect for and harmony with the situated reality in which we find ourselves in any given moment. Again, there may be harmony in protest, too. What is dangerous and ineffective is to ignore or deny the natural reality that presents itself to us while we concentrate on our own internal state. To be sure, our internal state is part of the circumstances of natural reality. But an exclusive focus on it ignores the rest of our situation and usually is accompanied by wishes that we felt (or were) different. There is so much relief when we learn to accept what is—all of what is—and get on with acting on it to make constructive changes.

14. REALITY IS A CLASSROOM.

Boredom usually results when people stop learning. When we are alert to pick up the lessons from moment-by-monent reality, there is no time for boredom. Education holds its existence in an attitude of readiness to learn and not in years of schooling, degrees, or encyclopedic knowledge. In the alert observation of people around us we can deduce some of the knowledge underlying their actions. We can learn from them without asking a single question. Morita suggested that we study our neurotic misery and learn from that, too. Access to understanding the principles of nature is open to anyone who studies reality diligently. Neurotic "symptoms," too, follow natural principles, however irrational and erratic they may appear at first.

Exclusive study of any single topic, however, leads to narrowness and insensitivity, as one sees in some elite university professors. The broad study of reality is what we are about.

15. FEAR WHAT IS FEARSOME.

You may find crowds frightening or it may be intimate relationships or the possibility of failure or apologies or being alone or losing control of your body or cockroaches or dirt or success or any of a vast array of things humans find upsetting. Morita advised that we go right ahead being afraid of what seems fearsome to us. There is no sense in trying to make the fear go away so that we can be fear-free, as we may mistakenly perceive others to be. The sensible thing to do about fear is to accept it and see if the fear prompts us to prepare or take measures for caution concerning the circumstances that provoke the fear. In other words, does the fear suggest something that needs doing?

Overcoming the fear doesn't mean doing away with it or becoming accustomed to it or learning to ignore it. Trouble appears for those who try to make the fear go away. The folks who suffer most are just those who try hardest to make themselves into what they are not. When we are scolded, we feel upset; when someone criticizes us, we feel some antagonism; when we are rejected, we

DAVID K. REYNOLDS

feel hurt—those responses are natural. They don't demonstrate any lack of humanity in us; they reaffirm our membership in the human race. In the same way, our fear response is part of our required equipment as humans. It is not an optional attachment that can be removed at will. What we *do* when we feel fear lies within our control, however. While feeling fear we can introduce ourselves, while trembling we can go shopping, while terrified we can commit our savings to a project, while perspiring we can take wedding vows, and so forth. Purposeful action in the presence of fear is what we mean by "overcoming the fear." Taking such action has produced new freedom for thousands and thousands of suffering people.

16. PILE UP EFFORT AND THE MIND CHANGES.

My clients would prefer instant cure. That's why many of them tried tranquilizers, antidepressants, sleeping pills, alcohol, and other drugs before coming to the ToDo Institute in Los Angeles, the Health Center Pacific on Maui, or similar places for help. The fact is that one grows a cure just as one grows a love; nobody buys these valuable conditions.

Morita likened the process to that of a chick hatching from an egg. Peck, peck, peck, peck, peck—and then new freedom. The effortful doing produces the results.

17. SELF-DEVELOPMENT FOR THE SAKE OF SELF-DEVELOPMENT.

In his day Morita, too, encountered what I call self-growth junkies. They are people who run from one trendy self-development process to another, sampling each, mastering none. In the Japan of sixty years ago most of the training possibilities were associated with religions. There seems to be a greater variety of possibilities, both religious and secular, in modern times. These days many such "junkies" are rather wealthy—it takes plenty of money to make the rounds as they do. Some of them are therapists.

They seem to be attached to the notion of tasting a variety of experiences. They get some satisfaction from having met the teachers, learning some of the terminology, talking about the principles. Morita called them a mistaken but interesting breed of human. He suggested that they would learn more from an intensive investment in one lifeway rather that flitting about here and there. I agree. Genuine understanding of a worthy lifeway comes with a long-term commitment of time and effort.

18. FOR THE GRADUATE OF THIS LIFEWAY, SUMMER IS HOT AND WINTER IS COLD.

Of course! And we feel shy when we feel shy, and we hurt when we hurt. All this is natural, ordinary, the way it is. The point Morita was making here was that people with a lot of neurotic moments tend to believe that there must be something wrong with their minds, that their minds must be operating on different psychological principles than the minds of other, "normal" people.

But they are wrong. Their main problem is that they don't recognize and accept the normal functioning of their minds. The heat makes them uncomfortable, so they focus on the discomfort rather than what needs doing. The shyness distracts them from normal social intercourse. Their efforts to make the natural feelings go away diverts them from normal everyday action. As graduates of the study of constructive living they learn to be hot when it is hot without any exclusive focus on their discomfort interfering with their lives.

Once more, it isn't that they learn to ignore the heat—how can anyone ignore it?—but the recognition becomes background to the foreground of studying or sweeping or shopping for an air conditioner.

19. FOND FOOLISHNESS.

The advanced students of constructive living, looking back on past symptoms, wonder how they could have been enveloped by such foolishness. Some even feel a sort of amused nostalgia for those days of the past. But for those still caught up in a neurotic consciousness any recollection of past symptoms brings only misery and the fear that hell will return again at any time.

20. SHARPENING OUR SAWS.

Morita pointed out the difference between the attitude of two of his students toward their neurosis. The first student was just beginning his study. He said that if only he hadn't been suffering from neurosis, he might have become a great person. The second student, advanced in his study, said that he was grateful for his neurosis because it led him to discover these fundamental principles of human living.

Morita commented that he watched a sawyer sharpen his saw three times in one day, taking forty minutes each time to accomplish the filing. It may seem like a waste of much time, but, in reality, that time was well spent. The time my students have spent suffering in neurotic misery have helped prepare them for the understanding about life that is available to them.

21. WHEN YOU'RE SUFFERING, DON'T CALL ON MORITA TO RESCUE YOU.

Some people try to cling to a teacher or a philosophical system to save them from their misery. Morita rejected any attempt to rely on him or his words to rescue anyone.

My students learn to incorporate the principles of this enhanced lifestyle into daily living by their own efforts. It isn't Morita's life or Reynolds's life that they are living. When the suffering begins to well up, they either accept it and get on about business, or they don't. To have to stop and invoke some memorized slogan or principle shows progress but also that there is a long way to go until graduation. When constructive activity flows naturally, without seeing it as anything special or anything learned in special circumstances, then "cure" is complete.

22. ANYONE WHO HAS BUMPED HIS SHIN DOESN'T NEED TO BE TOLD ABOUT THE PAIN; ANYONE WHO HASN'T CAN'T BE TAUGHT WHAT THE PAIN IS LIKE WITH WORDS.

By the time we are in our teens, we have had plenty of experience with the results of our actions. When we behaved selfishly, thoughtlessly of others, we have had the opportunity to see the results of our actions. When we have acted with consideration of others in spite of our selfish desires, there have been results for our observation. Put simply, reality has provided us with plenty of information about the results of self-centered, neurotic behavior. Whether we noticed the results or not is one issue; whether we acted on our observations or not is another.

We have either learned the lessons through experience or we haven't. Those who haven't learned at all are unlikely to be influenced by words.

23. THE DANGERS OF PRAISE AND SCOLDING.

Morita said that there is no need to praise oneself or others for doing what is ordinary and expectable. One of my clients remarked that this week he came out of his condominium for the first time in three years. My impulse is to praise him for that step, and sometimes praise slips out. But Morita was correct in objecting to such praise. Going out of one's house is ordinary behavior, unworthy of special comment. The rewards for nonneurotic behavior will be generated by reality, without the need for verbal praise (with the implied scolding, should the proper behavior cease). Similarly, reality provides natural punishment for self-limiting behavior. There is no need to scold a mature adult.

One of the problems of behavior-modification therapies when thoughtlessly applied is the danger that the client will become dependent on the artificially constructed rewards and punishments dealt out by the therapist. When the client leaves the therapy setting, there may be no carryover into everyday life. I don't want my students to associate doing well with praise from me. The doing well is reward enough in itself.

24. THERE IS MEANING IN THE SMALLEST TASK.

Ordinary people, once they get going on a task, can find some meaningfulness in it. The smallest household job, the tiniest editorial correction, the briefest mechanical adjustment—all hold some purpose. Neurotically sensitive persons may want to see some grand meaning in a task before undertaking it. They may want to know how it fits in with their overall cure or their entire future. If they cannot find some deep meaning, the task is beneath them; there must be something more important for them to be doing at the time. But they have no concrete alternative task at the moment, so they do nothing but sit and ponder what they should be doing. As a result, nothing gets done—neither large task nor small.

25. ADVICE ON OVERCOMING WRITER'S BLOCK.

Morita gave the following advice to a student who was having trouble writing a required paper: First, throw away any ideas about self-confidence or determination. You won't need them. Put your reading and writing materials in order on your desk. Sit down and engage in a patient staring contest with them. Several times a day for ten to thirty minutes at a time just sit at the desk. If you write a few lines, write them. If you open a book read it. Keep it up every day for a few weeks. Whether the writing goes well or not, whether you get into it or not, whether you like the sitting or not, don't stop. Don't let worries about courage, impatience, or confidence stop you.

Morita's experience was that the students who responded quickly began writing from about the second day, and those with more resistance held out about a week before the flow of writing began. Almost any activity is more attractive than hours of staring at blank paper.

The principles are clear and perfectly applicable to a variety of difficult tasks. We use behavior to keep ourselves in the situation for accomplishing the task. We sidestep the misleading effort to try to psyche ourselves up somehow. We prepare the materials. We wait for a predetermined period of time without allowing ourselves to get distracted by some other task. We keep bringing our bodies back to the task until we finish it.

26. DON'T GET CAUGHT UP IN AIRY PHILOSOPHICAL DEBATE. KEEP YOUR EYE ON REALITY.

In Morita's era, as in our own, neurotic students were fond of asking deep philosophical questions. "What is the purpose for my life?" "How can we distinguish between good and evil?" "How can I be sure that this task needs to be done?" "What are the relative influences of fate and effort in life?" "How can I be sure that this method will work for me?" "What is work?" "How do you define 'task,' 'reality,' 'natural'?" "What is the exact relationship between constructive living and Buddhism?" "Between constructive living and Christianity?"

It isn't that such questions have no importance. They are worthy of consideration. However, when asked by some students, they represent efforts to escape from the concrete reality of tasks at hand into drifting, unproductive speculation. During the teaching of constructive-living techniques we find it most helpful to keep referring the students back to concrete reality. Most of us know what needs to be done most of the time; too many of us have developed intellectualizing, fantasizing skills that distract us from what we know needs doing. The experienced Moritist guide won't be pulled into preoccupation with philosophical debate.

27. RESEARCH YOUR SYMPTOMS.

Morita suggested that we seriously and unflinchingly consider the conditions under which our anxieties and fears and self-doubts arise. Rather than the common rhetorical questions "Why is this unhappiness happening to me?" and "Where have I gone wrong?" and "When will this misery ever stop?" we are advised to observe our neurotic moments with the combination of a child's wonder and a researcher's objective eye.

To do so externalizes the symptoms. Although they lie within us, in a sense, the observation sets them apart—we become observers more than victims. Such purposeful observation leads us to consider actions to alleviate the circumstances that trigger our tensions and upset. Morita called this objective self-observation the starting point of cure. It is the starting point of cure in two senses: It both leads to change and is already change in itself.

28. FEELINGS ARE THE NATURAL RESPONSE TO EVENTS.

When people win lottery prizes, they are likely to feel joy. When we watch a fledgling teetering on a branch, we are likely to feel trepidation. When we scrape our elbows, we are likely to feel pain. Why need we single out some feelings (like sorrow, anger, apprehension, shyness, and anguish) as unnatural and worthy of elimination? They, too, are natural responses to certain conditions. They, too, are reflections of the world as seen through our eyes.

When we learn to stop struggling with these feelings directly and use our energies and time to make practical improvements in our circumstances, then the natural course of events is likely to lead to fewer unpleasant feelings. Moreover, when these "undesired" feelings appear, we are better able to take them in stride without being overwhelmed by them. Morita used words that may be translated "to stop discriminating" among feelings. He did *not* mean that we should try to achieve a state in which we cannot tell the difference between joy and pain. He did *not* mean that we should try to achieve a state in which we stop preferring joy to pain. He did mean that we must stop the useless discrimination that sets aside some feelings as unnatural and deserving of permanent banishment from our lives. There are no feelings like that. Our wishes and direct efforts by will to make any feeling go away only serves to intensify it. The process of this undesired intensification, too, is a natural process. In constructive-living study we ask nothing more than a clear look at reality and sensible action on the basis of what reality shows us.

29. THE STRATEGY IS SIMPLE, REQUIRING NO SUPERHUMAN EFFORT.

Morita wrote, "My way of doing things is simple. It's not necessary to make impossible efforts when troubled. Put simply, when you are vexed just by vexed and say, 'Yes, and what shall I do?' Just be in suspense about the outcome and move forward a little at a time."

Rarely is there any rush. Never is there any need to try to control feelings. When strong feelings such as anger are pouring forth, it is often wise to wait before acting. Strong emotions may interfere with clear thinking and careful consideration of the outcome of our actions. Given a few hours most emotions fade considerably, and those unusual ones that are still strong after half a day are signaling some very important event requiring our attention and, probably, some direct action.

30. THOSE WHO TAKE TIME IN THEIR SELF-DEVELOPMENT HAVE THE DEEPEST ROOTS.

Some people seem to have caught on to the principles of constructive living quickly. They show flashy changes in behavior quite rapidly. But the experience of struggle over time to change a student's view of the world is important in producing depth of character. Rapid progress sometimes produces a student who builds on success and not on the success-failure combination that reality is likely to present over the long run.

31. THE STRONGER THE DESIRE, THE STRONGER THE FEAR.

Those who want success most have the greatest fear of failure. Those who want good health most have the strongest fear of illness. A strong desire or need inevitably generates a corresponding anxiety about failure or loss in that area. We worry most about those we love, not about strangers.

There are a great number of strategies for dealing with this psychological reality. For example, the Buddhist strategy has been to try to do away with desire so that the accompanying anxiety is eradicated. The neurotic strategy is to try to keep the desire and eliminate the anxiety. The Christian strategy has been to try to turn over desires and corresponding anxieties to God. The psychoanalytic strategy has been to try to understand the sources of both desires and anxieties in the hopes of controlling them through understanding (through the rational ego). Morita suggested yet another alternative. That alternative is to accept the reality of this inevitable connection between desires and fears, to stop struggling with it, and to get on with living with the recognition that there is no escape from either desire or anxiety.

Such an existential position carries in itself neither optimism nor pessimism, no great meaning or great meaninglessness. It simply is the way things are. Now, what are we going to do next? The way one chooses from among these and other strategies is based on personal preference and one's circumstances, I suppose. But I strongly recommend getting an experiential taste of more than one strategy before making a commitment to any of them. Many of my students seem to have tried at one time or another in their lives the neurotic strategy of aiming for the desires without the anxieties. That seems to be a sort of default strategy for some people. It doesn't work.

32. THERE'S NO NEED TO COMPARE OURSELVES WITH WHAT WE THINK OTHERS ARE LIKE.

"Everybody else seems to be so together; I'm the only one who's uptight." Morita heard similar words in his day. We hear them far too often today. Many of my clients increase their suffering measurably by comparing themselves with the appearances of others. It hurts even more to be anxious about a final examination when all one's classmates seem so relaxed and confident as they enter the examination room. But the notion that "I alone suffer" is a patent falsehood based largely on a lack of understanding of the natural human condition.

Morita pointed out that others had been hit on the head by falling apples. Newton turned the painful experience into a contribution to science. Those without great doubts and great suffering are unlikely to produce great contributions to mankind. Rather than reflecting on the miserable quality of our lot as compared with others, there is more payoff in using our circumstances to produce something of value.

In Morita's opinion, success in business or in the academic world or in any practical pursuit is unlikely to be based on freedom from suffering. Instead, it is most likely to be built on three factors: an open mind, clear observation, and hard work.

33. DILEMMA AND PAIN ARE SOURCES OF PSYCHOLOGICAL GROWTH.

The gap between what we want and what is attainable creates tension and dissatisfaction. The effort and the mistakes we make in trying to close that gap teach us about ourselves in our world. In the confusion and error lie our chance for enlightened understanding. While failing we progress.

34. GIVING UP ON GETTING WELL IS THE PATH TO CURE.

I really prefer to use words other than medical terms like "cure" in the context of neurotic problems. But we have grown accustomed to talking about impractical living in medical terms. In Japanese, the term *naoru* means not only cure, but any kind of fixing or correcting—one can have one's car "cured" or "cure" a mispronounced word. In Japanese, the term that Morita used doesn't have an exclusively medical sense.

Morita was making the point here that certain kinds of thinking never lead to cure: "if only I could cure this anxiety, everything would clear up in my life" or "if I could get cured, all this misery would go away" or "I've got to get well so that I can lead a normal life." On the contrary, an attitude of "even if I get worse, it's all right" or "there's nothing wrong with staying neurotic the rest of my life" offers much more hope in leading to cure. What a paradox!

Sleep is the same, isn't it. The harder we try to make ourselves sleep, the harder it becomes. When we give up, the chances of sleeping increase considerably. It is the same with stuttering and some sexual dysfunctions. There is something about the pressure of attention that creates tension and reduces the chances of harmonious, smooth, natural functioning. Giving up offers our attention the possibility of turning outward, letting our inner functions take their natural course. We can begin to trust ourselves, even when we hurt ourselves.

Back in the 1920s when a person suffering from neurotic insomnia would come to this famous professor of Japanese medicine for help, Morita would tell the patient that it would have no effect on his health at all whether he slept or not. The patient would go home and sleep soundly for the first time in weeks. The next night the patient would have figured that the way to get himself to sleep is to cease to care about it one way or the other. So he would try to consciously create a state of mind in which he didn't care about

DAVID K. REYNOLDS

sleeping. Of course, he would be awake all night. Again, he was trying to force the sleep, this time using what he thought was a technique he learned from the doctor. I suspect that many people who read these pages will make similar attempts.

It is not only that trying to cure oneself doesn't lead to cure, but also that trying to cure oneself *is* neurosis at that very moment. In the same way, forgetting to work at cure is at that very moment cure itself. Those who have experiential understanding of these words know the essence of this constructive lifeway. The harder you try to make the suffering go away by your will, the further you are from relief.

One of my students in Los Angeles felt dizzy when eating at home but not when eating in restaurants. For six years she was unable to enjoy meals at home. She caught on to this principle of nonresistance after only two sessions and was amazed at the results. With her best efforts she was unable to even generate some dizziness when dining at home. The struggle against the possibility that dizziness might arise *was* the neurosis itself.

35. WHEN YOU BECOME INTERESTED IN OTHERS' CONVERSATION, YOU'RE ON THE ROAD TO CURE.

Morita noticed that some people came to his group meetings only with the intention of listening to material that would help them get cured. They tuned out when any other topic of conversation emerged. I know some people who read psychology and psychological self-help books exclusively, in the hopes of curing themselves. When the sole criterion about whether something is worth hearing (or worth reading) is how it relates to me and my problems, there is little chance that the listening will lead to a positive end.

36. BECOMING A WILLOW IN THE WIND.

Morita advised people who suffered from anxiety attacks to become willows in the wind. Just like the willow that bends with the breeze, they were not to oppose the panicky feelings that they were about to have a heart attack, that they were about to die.

Of course, regular physical checkups are necessary for anyone. But people with this condition have frequent attacks of desperation and anticipation of shortness of breath, chest pains, and sudden death in the presence of no genuine life-threatening physical malady.

Their attention is on how to keep the attacks from occurring, how to eliminate their fears, and how to keep themselves alive because-this-time-it's-real. The vital step toward cure for these people is, as expected, to stop fighting their condition. While fearful, while worried, they must bend like windblown willows but keep themselves firmly rooted in their ongoing activities. They must continue their doing without taking a break to joust with their feelings.

37. WISE PARENTS KEEP THEIR EYES ON REALITY.

Parents who give no guidance to their children and parents who pressure their children with too much guidance produce children who don't behave the way their parents prefer. In both extreme cases the parents are lost in their own thoughts. They fail to observe the reality that includes their own children. Constructive living emphasizes the need to keep on observing reality and learning from it. Reality includes children.

Parents who study their children learn about the children and about themselves. They modify their guidance to fit the needs of the child's circumstance rather than trying to apply some unthinking across-the-board abstract principles.

More than ten years ago I did a study of a young suicidal and psychotic man who allowed me to live alongside him for an extended period of time (Reynolds and Farberow, 1981). I observed and recorded what he did from the time he woke up until the time he went to bed. Of course, I tried to avoid being a strong influence on his life during the period of study. I ate when he ate, slept when he slept, entered and left rooms when he did, and so forth. The more I worked at understanding what Chuck was about, the more I found out about myself. I began to notice the way I send subtle signals to others that it is time to be ending a conversation, the way my body has become accustomed to taking nourishment at regular intervals, the amount and patterns of my sleep. As I tried to keep my behaviors under control so as to allow Chuck the maximum freedom possible, my usual habits became noticeable as they changed to fit Chuck's schedule. Chuck taught me about myself.

When we focus exclusively on ourselves, we learn little. The more we focus on what reality presents to us (as I focused on Chuck), the more we recognize the truth that the elements of reality, including our children, have much to teach us. We learn about reality and about ourselves as part of it.

38. JOY AND SORROW ARE LIKE THE SEASONS.

Summer is hot; winter is cold. Joy is wonderfully pleasant; sorrow is crushingly unpleasant. There is nothing we can do to make sorrow pleasant. We can't make ourselves enjoy grief or self-doubts or jealousy. There is nothing directly to be done about these aspects of reality except to acknowledge them and to live within their bounds. Even with the steadiest of behavior and the best of luck we won't escape their influence at times in our lives.

39. PUT YOUR BODY IN A BUSY ENVIRONMENT.

People who are constantly self-conscious and uptight would do well to put their bodies in a busy environment, Morita advised. The advice holds true today. In busy circumstances we have a greater chance of being pulled into activity. Lying on the couch at home alone increases the chances of even further inactivity. Inactivity breeds inactivity.

The shy, self-conscious individual feels some relief by retreating from a busy, active workplace in society. But more constructive relief comes from getting caught up in business or play activity within a more social environment.

We become more interesting speakers and writers by getting out in the world, not by sitting idly at a desk or practicing long periods of meditation, said Morita. The human mind needs to move about to refresh itself. Morita called the active, seeking mind "the mind that lives nowhere." Its natural state is to be constantly on the move with a sort of light alertness.

When we become active in our world, we find much to learn. When our attention wanders to some current obsession, we lose the alert flow of attention to the moment's reality and nick our finger while peeling the apple. This lesson cannot be learned by sitting comfortably at home with pen in hand. A variety of situations create a variety of learning experiences and a variety of selves for development.

40. THE BIGGER THE DIFFICULTY, THE BIGGER THE ENLIGHTENMENT.

I'm not sure that Morita meant "enlightenment" in a strictly Zen sense. There are some Moritists who hold that he did, and some who disagree. Since many modern-day Moritists are repelled by the religious trappings of Zen in Japan, they are unlikely to have intimate knowledge of fundamental Zen enlightenment with which to compare Morita's enlightenment. It matters not at all, however, because the enlightenment Morita wrote about is worth experiencing in its own right.

Freedom is gradually stifled by neurotic symptoms. More and more aspects of life fall under their sway. Those who suffer find themselves making more and more accommodations to their self-imposed limitations. When the principles of constructive living take root in these compacted lives of misery, there is a tremendous sense of new freedom, a new perspective on life. And the greater the initial pain, the greater the contrast with the recognition of release. The greater the difficulty, the greater the enlightenment.

Morita pointed out that we learn the value of good health when we become ill. Furthermore, troubles prompt us to reexamine our current understandings and assumptions about the world. Not all neurotics achieve enlightenment, but their suffering provides fertile ground for a closer look at feelings, awareness, behavior, purpose, and so forth. The freedom that comes from enlightenment goes beyond the freedom that existed before the neurotic narrowing of life. It is not a return to a previous state. It is something new made possible by the suffering. Recognition of this potential allows the graduate of constructive living to actually be grateful to the old neurotic lifestyle that made enlightenment in this sense possible.

41. THE DEAFNESS OF NEUROTIC PEOPLE.

Anyone who works with shinkeishitsu oversensitive people sometimes finds frustration in their lack of capacity to listen. Morita wrote that you can say to a neurotic that both the sun and the moon are round and he will say, "But the sun's light is stronger, so they're different." Or you can say that sometimes the student hears the ticking of the wall clock and sometimes not, at which point the student will say, "But I'm bothered by my eyes, not my ears."

This countering tendency prevents the neurotic person from hearing the truth of what others say. It also works internally to forestall straightforward action by the suffering individual. Neurotics counter their own thoughts and arguments, too, leaving themselves paralyzed by indecision. "I could do this, but then that might happen," "I'd like to try this, but then I'd be prevented from trying that," "I've been following this course of action, but do I really want to be doing this?" and so forth.

There is a fine word in Japanese, sunao, translated in some dictionaries as "mild" or "obedient." It implies a sort of pure acceptance, without a trace of resistance. Neurotics don't show such a sunao quality toward the words of others, toward their own thought processes and feelings, toward reality. Their struggling is their neurosis. Once again, it is important to emphasize that sunao acceptance doesn't imply passivity. Not only can the fine swordsman accept his opponent with "sunao-ness" and still conquer him; he must do so in order to win. The slightest resistance to the opponent's style interferes with the smooth flow of response.

In my former basketball days we sometimes tried to bait our opponents into anger so that they were playing against their own anger as well as against us. Wise and experienced opponents saw the baiting for what it was, accepted it, and scored baskets. We were caught trying to play basketball and bait our opponents at the same time. The dual purposes distracted us from our game. We ended up resisting, and losing, when our opponents were sharp enough to avoid resisting our tactics.

Not only does this countering tendency interfere with listening, but also the neurotic's self-centeredness produces deaf ears. Psychoanalysis caters to the tendency of neurotics to want to talk about themselves. They are filled with complaints that they pour out on others at the slightest opportunity. Whatever they hear triggers some self-reference, some connection with their own pain in contrast to the apparent well-being of those folks around them. It isn't surprising that the important people in their lives eventually become irritated at having to listen to a stream of selfish negativity. The pressure to complain prevents the neurotic person from being a sensitive listener. Neurotic habits push the individual toward social and psychological isolation.

42. JUST PUT THE PRINCIPLES INTO ACTION AND SEE THE RESULTS.

Just try and see, Morita advised. There's no need to understand some complex theory. I see not a few clients who are tired of trying to make sense of what their former psychotherapist was doing. The neurotic wants to figure it all out beforehand.

Constructive action isn't planless or purposeless. Nevertheless, the plans and purposes may not be abundantly clear before an exercise or assignment is undertaken. Understanding unfolds as the prescribed activity is carried out. Those who follow through on the activities reap the benefits. Intellectual satisfaction is subordinate to pragmatic results.

43. CURE OF NEUROSIS LEADS TO THE POSSIBILITY OF REPENTANCE.

Repentance and existential guilt are conditions that Western psychotherapies try to eliminate. Such a goal is based on the unfortunate misunderstanding that some feelings are bad, wrong, worthy of erasure. Fortunately, no one is very successful at elim-

DAVID K. REYNOLDS

inating unpleasant feelings (except through strong drugs that produce very unsatisfactory side effects on the bodymind).

Repentance and guilt are necessary and healthy, however unpleasant and disturbing they feel. As with any feelings, we run into trouble when we try to resist or destroy them. Some neurotic symptoms seem to be tied in to suppressing feelings of guilt. Be that as it may, the recognition of one's past hurtful actions toward others, the desire to confess and to make restitution, are natural tendencies in anyone with human sensitivity. As always, feelings offer information that deserves consideration when we evaluate what needs to be done.

Confession in the proper circumstances to a trusted confidant is beneficial. Action to counter the effects of one's past selfishness is extremely helpful whenever possible. When past mistakes can't be corrected through reconstructive action (when a parent has died, for example), then we must work to repay those we live with today for our mistakes of yesterday. What else can we do?

Repentance implies an acknowledgment of the needs of others, the needs we failed to take into consideration. The neurotic person is so self-centered that considerable progress toward cure is necessary before healthy guilt and repentance emerge in some recognizable form. Constructive living has borrowed and modified methods from a Japanese therapy form called Naikan (see Reynolds, 1983) to help in recognition and repayment of our debt to the world. The result is an upwelling awareness that we are loved and supported in concrete ways in every moment. With that awareness comes gratitude and a new purposefulness underlying constructive action.

We noted before that opposites imply and contain each other. Here, too, we find that the depth of the guilt is reflected in the depth of the gratitude, the depth of recognition that we are loved is reflected in the depth of the desire to serve others. In other words we need the guilt for the gratitude, we need the awareness of being loved to love. Such an assertion may seem strange, but, again, it isn't necessary to understand or to believe it. In the doing lies experiential understanding.

Morita outlined the following three-step program for a person suffering from writer's cramp. I'll show how the principles can be generalized to any similar problem. In this case, the client's hand trembled when he picked up a pen or brush, causing the characters to be ugly and, often, illegible. The client tried to avoid writing, particularly in the presence of others. Perhaps I should note here that in Japan, even to some degree today, one's penmanship is seen as a reflection of character. People make social and psychological judgments on the basis of handwriting. Such an attitude is not altogether foreign to us in the West. I evaluate a messy, scrawled note differently from a neatly penned missive. Perhaps you do, too. Now to the program:

1. Hold the pen as you would normally. Don't make any adjustments to try to correct the trembling and tension in the fingers.
2. Recognize and acknowledge your lack of skill in this area. Write as clearly as you can.
3. Don't practice writing. Write when the natural occasion arises, without avoiding such occasions.

Put in more general terms, Morita was advising that (a) we avoid taking artificial stances to shore up (or to conceal) our neurotic handicaps; (b) while acknowledging our problem, we conduct our actions as best we can; and (c) we operate in natural circumstances with natural purposes. The last point has to do with the difference between doing our best in situations as they arise versus creating settings in which practice is the purpose. Our most useful and flexible skills seem to develop best as by-products of our activities in a variety of contexts.

The underlying taken-for-granted worldview here involves the aim of "naturalness." I point out these underlying assumptions from time to time because I think that prospective clients, students, and guides should be aware of the basic building blocks on which a therapeutic system is erected. In this case, Morita recommends a natural grasping of the pen, a natural recognition of limitations, and a natural circumstance for the writing. A neurotic approach prods toward an artificial grip (holding the pen closer to the point for more control), artificial thinking (putting the problem out of one's mind, attacking the mental problem, generating confidence), and an artificial situation (scaled practice, rehearsal in a sheltered setting).

45. LEARNING TO VALUE OUR NEUROTIC MOMENTS AS THOUGH THEY WERE PEARLS.

Pearls aren't opals, and they're not rubies. They have their own value, their own beauty. We can learn to accept ourselves as we are in any moment and work to polish the beauty that lies within us without wishing we were opals or rubies.

46. QUITTING ONE'S JOB SHOULD BE AVOIDED.

Morita saw quitting work as a great tragedy for neurotically sensitive people. They may think that after straightening out their lives they will return to work. But for many the structure and purposefulness of the work was helping to hold them together. Morita wrote that he never advised anyone to stop working.

I have seen shinkeishitsu clients deteriorate after they decided to leave their jobs and stay home to rest and recuperate from their self-consciousness. Retreating to isolation results in more focus on the symptoms and further decrements in constructive action. The problems actually increase with long hours in bed. Generally speaking, our bodies see that we get enough sleep and rest. Usually, the best break involves changing from one activity to another, not stopping from activity altogether. When I become tired by reading or writing, I switch to more physical work. When Morita became chronically ill in his old age, he largely determined his activity on the basis of his body temperature. Up to a certain temperature he wrote. When his temperature rose above a certain point, he read. With still higher temperatures he had someone read to him. He allowed circumstance to dictate his activity, but there was allowance for flexibility when visitors came and deadlines approached. This example may seem somewhat compulsive to some, but I find his attempt to objectify one aspect of his life situation (by means of a thermometer reading), and to adapt himself to it, quite admirable given the limiting circumstances of his illness.

When the pressures of work are too great or the job unbearably uninteresting, I advise my clients to find other work before leaving their current place of employment. It may be unwise to resign in order to look for another position.

47. WHEN A CHILD SEES A SOLDIER'S GOLD BRAID, THE CHILD WANTS TO BECOME A SOLDIER. BECOME LIKE A CHILD.

Some of my clients say that they have no interests, no hobbies, no desire to make effort in life, no desire to study anything. Morita suggested to such people that they just attend to anything upon which their eye falls.

He wrote that when a child sees a soldier's gold braid, the child wants to become a soldier. Riding on a ferry, the child wants to become a ship's captain; hearing about Edison, the child wants to become an inventor; and so forth. In each new circumstance the child's interest emerges spontaneously. There is no effort on the child's part to create some interest or to maintain some long-term interest. The child just identifies with what is encountered in a particular time and place.

Perfectionistic, self-driving people may hamper their natural interests by believing that they ought to have interests in certain areas, that certain kinds of curiosity are wrong, childish, or beneath them. Putting our mindbodies in a variety of physical locations maximizes the chances of allowing a variety of interests. We cannot force an interest, but we can provide ripe opportunities for its spontaneous emergence.

48. LACK OF CONFIDENCE IN SHINKEISHITSU NEUROTICS ISN'T OFTEN BASED ON REALITY.

Morita wrote that in his student days he and his friends would get together and talk about upcoming examinations. His friends seemed to know a lot of material. He felt worried that he knew so little and dreaded taking the exam. After the exam was over, his friends would be talking about having written three or four pages of essays while he had been writing only one or two. As a result, Morita felt no confidence about succeeding in these tests.

The odd thing was that when the grades were posted, he usually had the best scores. If his friends scored in the seventies the young Morita scored in the eighties. The reality was that his friends talked beforehand only about what they knew, and they wrote on their exams more than necessary, about irrelevant material.

The immature person builds a self-image based on the appearances of others. Comparison of one's own weakness with the apparent strengths of others will quite expectably produce feelings of inferiority. Getting on with doing the best we can puts such unfavorable comparisons out of mind.

49. IT'S AMAZING HOW DIFFERENT THE WORLD LOOKS WHEN WE HAVE CHANGED.

As a more positive lifestyle develops, we begin to see the kindness and love of others. It may appear that they have changed drastically, but, more likely, it is just that our eyes have turned outward from the old neurotic inner focus. There is no question that our new behavior affects those around us. Our loved ones are likely to find it easier to love us and show us kindness as we take on our share of life's tasks and responsibilities. But the love and services were there before, we just didn't notice them.

50. ENLIGHTENMENT IS ACTING REALISTICALLY.

When Morita's students went into the garden, they could find nothing to do. They stood around bored, even though the flowers were in need of water.

The students of today are the same. They may not be in a garden. What needs doing may not be to water the flowers. But they fail to notice what reality has brought for them to do. They fail to act realistically. So, naturally, they fail to develop a love for reality. If your room is untidy, straighten it. If your friend needs a word of encouragement, speak up. What does the world need from you?

51. WE AREN'T FRUGAL IN ORDER TO SAVE MONEY; WE PRESERVE THINGS BECAUSE THEY DESERVE OUR CARE.

When we take this view of reality seriously, the objects of reality cannot be used wastefully. Environmental protection is not a new concept. We use the simplest of materials carefully, gratefully. A new car and a piece of tissue paper, a personal computer and the stub of a pencil—each has its value. Each deserves to be used in its time, with attention and respect for its contribution to accomplishing what needs doing.

The purpose of economizing for some people has become the empty goal of accumulating money. Money, too, has its place in accomplishing moment-by-moment tasks. But money remains only one aspect of reality's treasures. The treasures are there to be seen . . . when the eyes are open.

PART III

TALES

MWWWW

MWWWW

MWWWW

Balloon Boy

Not so long ago, in a land not far from here, lived a six-year-old boy named Homma. He was a normal lad in every way except that when he held his breath, the air made him swell up like a balloon. In a few seconds he became as big and as strong as the strongest man, just by holding his breath. Of course, after a few minutes he would have to exhale. Then all the air would be expelled, and Homma's body would become that of an ordinary six-year-old again.

His mother was terrified. When he was big, he would threaten her. A few times he even hit her, leaving angry red marks on her face and arms. When he let out his breath and became little Homma again, the red marks remained on his mother's body. They were reminders of his awful power.

Homma's mother did everything she could to keep her son from becoming angry and hurting her. She watched him closely to see when he wanted to eat or what toy he might want to play with next. As soon as she saw that he might want something, she hastened to bring it to him.

Homma soon learned that his mother was watching him closely. So he suddenly shouted out, "I want strawberries!" in the middle of winter right after breakfast. He wanted to see if his mother would try to get him everything he wanted, even without any warning and even if what he wanted was very hard to get. Another time he rolled on the floor pretending his stomach was hurting. "I need a doctor quick! I want that sweet orange medicine! You gave me something rotten to eat! You made me sick!"

His mother rushed out feeling afraid and guilty, trying to find a doctor and medicine on a Sunday afternoon.

Homma's demands were hard to fulfill, but his mother could usually manage something. Sometimes, however, Homma gave his mother impossible tasks. "I want an ice-cream cone, but don't leave my room!" "Stop being afraid of me!" "Make the water run back into the tub from the drain!" "Fix this dead spider so it lives again!" When Homma asked his mother for something impossible, she sat down and cried, trembling with fear. Usually he would hit her anyway.

Remember that Homma was only a boy of six. There were lots of things he couldn't do for himself—things he didn't know how to do or wasn't old enough to do or simply was too lazy to do for himself. So he depended on his mother for many, many services. Strangely, he especially wanted precisely those things his mother couldn't provide. He wanted so very much just what his mother couldn't give him.

So Homma hated his mother.

She couldn't give him what he most wanted. She couldn't grant him the impossible. Homma forgot about all the nice things she worked so hard to produce for him. He remembered only what she failed to produce. And so he hated her.

Homma was filled not only with anger and hate but also with sadness and disappointment. All the things he most wanted he couldn't have. How sad.

When he realized the extent of his dilemma, he refused to leave his room—for weeks. When grownups came to ask him to go to school or to clean up the trash that accumulated in the room, he simply swelled up and threatened them until they went away. He cried a lot.

Although Homma's mother still feared her son, she also worried about his health and his sorrow. She wanted to see him happy again. She tried everything she could think of to cheer him up, but nothing seemed to work. Even when he hit her, he didn't seem to find relief.

Homma's dilemma finally reached the newspapers. Reporters came to interview the family. Little Homma stayed in his room and refused to talk with them.

A few days later a neatly dressed old man came to the door of Homma's house. When asked his business there, he replied, "I can make your son happy again."

"How?" Homma's mother asked.

He told her. At first she didn't understand how the old man's plan could help her son. She had tried so many complicated ways that might have worked but didn't. Perhaps this strangely simple plan would be effective.

They tied a belt around Homma's chest and buckled it in the back. He wore this belt every day for a year and became a very happy boy.

You see, the belt stopped him from taking in a big breath. It stopped him from becoming a powerful man with a child's desires. He was just little Homma. Now his mother could tell him no on occasion and he listened; he couldn't blow himself up to threatening size.

Even with the belt around his chest little Homma wasn't entirely helpless. He used all the wiles of crying and whining and pouting and yelling that every little kid can use. But his power was balanced by his mother's power. He stopped asking for the impossible, and soon he stopped wanting it.

He is now a well-adjusted boy of seven. During this period he seems to have outgrown his ability/curse to become gigantic, so the belt around his chest isn't necessary anymore. His mother still keeps a close eye on him to see what he wants and needs. Now she is no longer afraid of the consequences of failure. She *likes* to provide for him. She even seems to love him more now that he's not so strong.

This story is about a boy and his mother, about some husbands and wives, about some patients and therapists, about nations and other subjects. It is a story about dissatisfaction. Homma was unhappy because he had power to control his mother. He found more satisfaction when the power was balanced better. Unbalanced power was driving Homma crazy. He needed limits to discover sanity and freedom. How can we love anyone whom we control? How can we love anyone who controls us?

By the Way

In a far kingdom a greengrocer had three sons. The eldest son lacked courage. So the greengrocer sent him out to find someone who could give him courage. The son was given some money and told not to return home until three years had passed in his quest to find a proper teacher of courage.

The second son lacked persistence. The greengrocer set him the task of working in the store as an apprentice for three years in order to save enough money to pay for psychological treatment that would make him more persistent.

The third son lacked purpose. So his father ordered him to study for three years in order to discover a worthy purpose.

At the end of three years the eldest son returned home. He returned with courage even though he hadn't encountered someone to give it to him. The second son had saved enough money for psychotherapy, but he no longer needed help developing persistence. The third son found a purpose within the three years, but the purpose wasn't written in a book. He became a scholar.

Morita noted that by the time some people had worked to save up enough money for private inpatient treatment, they no longer needed it. The diligent, purposeful working itself had worked the "cure." So often it is in the doing and not in the being-done-to that we change in most important ways.

DAVID K. REYNOLDS

Chains

Samuel shuffled around the village with shackles about his ankles. From morning until evening you could tell where he was making firewood deliveries by the clanking sounds of the chains he wore. In his leather coat and apron, his hair neatly cropped, with a load of branches on his back, and those everpresent chains restricting his gait, he was quite a sight to behold.

Surprisingly, the chains were polished and gleaming each morning as he left his house. Even more surprisingly, Samuel wore the shackles voluntarily. He was the one who put them on in the first place. His story isn't well known, but it goes like this:

Ten or twelve years ago, Samuel woke up and headed outside to stretch and discover the day. As he set foot across the doorstep, he stumbled over dirty, rusted shackles. How they came to be on Samuel's doorstep no one knew (the story of who put them there and why is for another time and place). Certainly, he had done nothing to deserve them. His first impulse was to ask around town to find the rightful owner. But, then, who would claim such rusty old impediments? It would be tantamount to admitting some past crime, for only criminals wore such "leg necklaces." No, no one would claim them. No one wanted them.

Samuel had the odd notion that the chains had been given specifically to him. But if they had been made for him, why did they appear so old and rusted? The locks were open. The cuffs fit his ankles perfectly. Without really considering all the implications of what he was about to do, Samuel slipped the locks through their fittings and snapped them shut. Then he shuffled around the living room getting the feel of the things. And for some odd reason he kept them on.

In the days that followed sores developed on his feet from the banging and chafing of the chains. There were days when he considered trying to work his legs free from the metal wraps, but he knew he could not. As weeks passed, his legs and feet toughened. He became accustomed to the limitation of movement.

He began to polish the chains.

It was about that time that several bright young men came to discuss the matter with Samuel. They told him they could rid him of his chains for a certain amount of money. It might take time, but wouldn't he prefer to walk unfettered? But Samuel decided to keep them on. They fit him.

As the months passed, he wore the shackles proudly, whether they were gleaming in the morning or dusty as they dragged home in the dust of the evening streets.

In that small village it became a sort of custom for young people to imitate Samuel by decorating themselves with little silver shackles about their ankles. The shackles became jewelry.

The shackles have grown thin in places now. They could easily be broken. Samuel's legs are thick and strong from carrying the extra weight each day. He hardly notices the metal burden. There is no need to break the chains. Someday, perhaps, they will fall off by themselves.

Life sometimes presents us with responsibilities and obligations that hamper our freedom. An elderly, bedridden parent, a disabled child, a mentally disordered spouse, a failing business, a chronic injustice—all these are examples of situations that can place unexpected shackles on our time and movement. Some people have grown strong through these circumstances. Some, like Samuel, have learned to make even their chains bright and shining.

DAVID K. REYNOLDS

Cleverlessness

In a distant country there lived a man who had the world all figured out. He thought like this: She can't be bright because she is pretty. He can't be deep because he is humorous. That teacher can't be knowledgeable because he is young. That advice can't be therapeutic because it is so simple and understandable.

The man never read a best-seller, never took medicine that tasted good, never drove a popular model car, never conversed with a rich man. If something looked good, he figured it must be bad. He liked movies about bad cops and bad preachers and good whores and soft-hearted criminals.

There were people who could have told him that his system of evaluation wasn't superior or clever; it was just narrow. It was as limited as following the crowd, buying what has the biggest advertising budget, living by horoscope. We all look for ways to pare down the choices we must make each day. Some ways are better than others. Someone could have told him that truth. But, then, would he have listened?

Needless to say, we live in a complex world. We carry with us all sorts of stereotypes and maxims and other tactics to make our personal worlds more manageable for us. Our brains do a great deal of channeling and simplifying the storm of stimuli that floods us before we are even aware of our sensory experience. There is so much going on in reality.

We must be careful to examine our tactics of simplification now and again. There is genuine payoff in pulling ourselves closer to reality. Our styles of organizing our world may lead to unnecessary misery and unnecessary limitations on ourselves and the people around us.

DAVID K. REYNOLDS

Control

"Henry, get me a roller, will you? No, not *that* one, the one over there."

"This one, Ma?"

"Yes, dear. Now the other one. Yes, that one. Just a minute. Where are you going so fast? While my hands are full, wipe up that mess your sister made on the counter. That girl! Just spills and goes. Not a thought about the trouble she causes her mother. . . . Oh yes, Henry?"

"Yes, Ma."

"The trash needs to be put out for tomorrow."

"Okay, Ma. Can I go to Arnie's house then?"

"Be home at five-fifteen, no later. And take a sweater. Your nose is running already. Blow it before you go. What would Arnie's mother think of me, letting you out with a runny nose."

"Yes, Ma."

Henry fled to Arnie's house. There he and Arnie were engaged in a dog-training project. They were teaching Snowwhite to obey certain commands. Snowwhite wasn't very bright, but the big furry creature didn't have the heart to actively resist them. The boys were pretty satisfied with their progress so far.

Not surprisingly, Henry joined the army after high school and went away to far lands. Some of his mother's letters went unopened, unread; nearly all went unanswered. In the army Henry learned the military version of who deserved unquestioned obedience and who could be ignored. Henry didn't mind army life. It seemed rather familiar.

After his tour of duty Henry worked as an apprentice cook in a string of restaurants. As a novice he was ordered about by the other cooks and even by aggressive waiters. A disagreement with the boss always resulted in his quitting or being fired. Henry was never clear about whose orders were absolute and whose were unworthy of concern in the restaurant business. He worked toward the day when he could be head chef and take orders from nobody.

When he became head chef, he was puzzled to discover that there were still people with authority over him, limiting his budget, selecting his menu, and so forth. He could not escape the softly worded commands.

Henry stayed far away from his hometown during those years. But his mother pulled him back home for Christmas each year. He endured those few days, in part, because of his loneliness.

When Henry began psychotherapy, he was careful to choose the kind of person he wanted as therapist—someone who wouldn't push him around. He set the time of the therapy session at 7:00 A.M. He set the fee, the rules about what assignments he would carry out; he determined who would talk and when.

For a time, therapy was enjoyable for Henry. But after a few sessions he got tired of moving his therapist about and finding no resistance. He began to see the burden involved in controlling others, the attention and energy it requires. He began to see another side of his mother. He wrote a letter thanking her for the trouble she had gone to in raising him.

He got a prompt reply to his letter inviting him to spend Easter, too, at home that year. It was only a couple of weeks away. Henry *chose* to visit his home for Easter and *allowed* his mother to maneuver him about that weekend. He thoroughly enjoyed the visit!

During the flight back to the West Coast Henry fell asleep and dreamed that he was a child playing in a sandbox with a big puddle of water in the center. Water trickled down the channel he had dug in the sand. He tried and tried to pile up sand to stop the flow, but the water slowly backed up until it overflowed his sand banks. Suddenly, he got the idea of digging a new channel upstream to divert the flow. It worked beautifully. Henry clapped his sandy hands together with glee.

Being influenced or controlled may not be so bad in every situation. Choosing to allow the control for clear purposes puts one's destiny back into one's own hands. Giving ourselves away to others may involve allowing them some limited influence over us. We Americans have been taught to value fierce independence. A satisfying life, however, fits reality and not some idealized model of inflexibility.

Deafening

"How's your new hearing aid, Mrs. Vincent?" I asked.

"I'm just fine; and how are you?" she replied.

"Is your hearing aid working all right?"

"Sonny, I haven't worked for years." She smiled benevolently at my stupidity.

Mrs. Vincent refuses to believe she has a hearing problem. She insists she got the hearing aid merely because her friends were pressuring her to do so. Despite clear messages from her dearest friends and from her grown children, the gray-haired, pin-curled lady won't recognize the reality that presents itself to her.

This tale is based on an actual conversation I had with a dear lady in the lobby of the building in which we both live.

None of us relishes taking a clear, cool look at our own limitations and faults. But reality is persistent. It keeps reminding us through a variety of means in a variety of situations what needs our attention and effort to improve.

DAVID K. REYNOLDS

Filling Up the Valley

Many years ago there was a long rope bridge spanning a deep valley. No one knew how the bridge had been put in place or who had put it there. One night during a violent windstorm the bridge was torn apart and flung away. Only its distant, tattered ends remained in the morning.

From that day one villager began to haul rocks to the top of the cliff overlooking the valley. The climb was steep and his load was heavy, but day after day he pushed and lugged hundreds of pounds of rocks to the clifftop and pushed them over the edge. They tumbled down onto the valley floor. Some of them were caught by the river and carried farther downstream.

Many of the villagers scoffed at this man's futile efforts. "You will never make a new bridge that way," they laughed. "How can anyone fill up such a vast expanse? It would take hundreds of years and hundreds of men to even begin to show some results. Look! The river carries away most of your effort anyway." They shook their heads at his foolishness.

Certainly, the loss of the bridge caused them much inconvenience. They had to carry their trade goods down the side of the valley, across the river, and up the other side to get to the local market. Nevertheless, this fellow's work was sheer foolishness! It would never change the conditions appreciably.

Yet he toiled on, day after day, month after month, year after year. Some days as he looked down into the valley, it looked as though a small pile of rocks had begun to form. On other days he could see no results of his efforts at all. Yet he continued with his task.

If you asked him why he carried on with such a fruitless task, he might have mumbled something about his desire to do something about the broken bridge, about the added suffering caused the villagers by the difficult trip to market. It was hard to find words for the restlessness he would feel if he weren't doing something, however trivial, about the problem.

One day this unnamed man died as he pushed a heavy boulder up the mountainside. Looking down into the valley, one could see little effect of his years of labor. Still, his face looked peaceful in death. Where there might have been a grimace from the exertion of years of effort there was only a smile.

There are many similar stories in Zen literature. One such tale is that of a small bird who tries to put out a blazing forest fire with the water it can carry on its wings.

Many important and worthwhile life tasks show no apparent results. We must undertake them not because we can accomplish them in our lifetime but because they are worthy of our effort. Working to relieve human misery is one such task. The satisfaction is in the doing.

The End Result

The first advertisement appeared in the *Los Angeles Times*. It announced a new service for people who were near the end of their lives. Anyone who was terminally ill or planning to commit suicide or just tired of living could take advantage of this service. They were invited to sacrifice themselves for humanity. Meaningful Risk was the name of the service organization. It provided a referral to dangerous and distasteful jobs that could be done by someone in the mood for self-sacrifice.

Within weeks there were full-page ads in leading newspapers across the country. Some were surprised to learn that the phones at Meaningful Risk were so busy that extra operators had to be hired to handle the calls.

Feature stories began to appear in less than a month. Arnie Gender, dying of terminal cancer, threw the switch that executed Ostermann, a convicted murderer. Gender said that no one should have to live a long life knowing that they had been the final cause of another human's death. He had only a few weeks to live. He would carry that burden for the rest of humanity.

Two quadriplegics risked their lives in fifty-mile-per-hour auto crashes to test new safety devices. Lars Friel, age eighty, was living alone and ready to commit suicide. His repair work prevented a nuclear meltdown but cost him his life from the radiation. "I ain't much, but what I am I'll give to my country."

Clara Carpenter allowed her own immune system to be eradicated so that her organs could be donated to several other patients without rejection. She died within a week. Several known gangland leaders were shot and suicidal attacks on drug dealers and pimps were reported, but these incidents couldn't be directly traced to Meaningful Risk.

Military forces created small, specialized units for "one-way" missions. Medical experimentation with dangerous drugs and procedures progressed remarkably due to the carefully screened pool of volunteers from Meaningful Risk.

The American public felt gratitude for all the positive results of these efforts. But there was also a curiosity and some suspicion in the minds of many. Surely, this endeavor had the potential for abuse. People were risking their health, their very lives, in these Meaningful Risk ventures. Were they properly informed of the possible consequences of their acts? Were they being coerced into cooperation? Could they be counseled out of their suicidal wishes? Could they be saved from their severe illnesses by heroic medical efforts? Were there alternatives to risking their lives for society? The phones at Meaningful Risk kept ringing.

Purpose and meaning have power in human life beyond our ordinary expectations. Tragedies of loss pull from us the urge to find meaning in the reality that presents itself to us. We grieve because our dying friend or relative will be lost to us. A dying person grieves because everyone and everything will be lost. We all are forced to search for purpose and meaning in death.

Fearflies

Once upon a misty morning a fairy flew across the wide ocean to escape from her own fearflies. Of course, the fearflies followed her, because they belonged to her.

"Go away!" she cried. "You make me feel tiny and uncomfortable. I have no need of your services. Return to my homeland, and I shall stay in exile on this tropical island. Please, leave me alone!"

The fearflies looked like tiny lightning bugs flickering about her silvery fairy wings. They spoke to her in unison, with a buzzing voice, a strangely monotone voice. But their words were clear.

"You are wrong," they buzzed. "You need us for your existence as much as we need you for ours. You are our home. We are your protectors."

"But how can you be my protectors if you protect me from all the things I want in life?" wailed the little fairy. "You make me fear people and fairies and flying and even myself. Begone, all of you! I need no fears!"

"Please," buzzed the fearflies, "listen to us. We can live together without quarreling. Truly, we are here to serve you. Don't you remember that odd magic wand that nearly electrocuted you when you touched it? Remember how we circled around it whenever you drew near to remind you of the danger it held. Remember how we prodded you to prepare adequately for speech before the Court of Elves. You take vitamins and go for physical checkups because of our buzzing. Without us you would have long ago blown away on the wind to where the milkweed flies. Can't you see that we are a help to you?"

"Yes, but you present only one side of the case. I find it hard to see you objectively. You cause tension and misgiving in my world. That is what I hate."

"Perhaps we could come to some agreement. We need you. You need us."

And so they did. The fearflies continued to fly wherever they pleased, but they agreed to buzz more clearly about the objects of their interest. The fairy agreed to respect and appreciate the fearflies, but she reserved the right to turn to other things after acknowledging their insistent messages. The fearflies became her pets.

This story was written for a mildly phobic young lady who flew to Maui to try to escape from her fears on the Mainland. She was treated briefly at the Health Center Pacific.

Viewing our emotions (in this case, our fears) as natural companions—neither good nor bad, neither to be eliminated nor to be overencouraged—capable of providing us with information and flavor in our world, is a key to living constructively and sensibly.

DAVID K. REYNOLDS

A Garden to Tend

Becky's parents died and left her a large, luxurious garden. It was sufficient to support her for the rest of her life, they thought. They died peacefully, knowing they had given her the best they could.

Becky worked diligently in the garden. She raised fine crops year after year, enough to make a comfortable living at first. No one anticipated the seasons of drought one after another, the torrential rains that drove the soil into the river, the alkali that made her vegetables more and more bitter as the years passed. Becky struggled with the land. She banked the soil, hoed and weeded and scraped out a meager living for a few more years. Then she felt she could go on no longer.

By then she was an adult. She was tired of the everyday wrestling match with the elements. She longed to become a child again. She desperately wanted a safe, warm, happy space for herself—a child's simple self-centered existence—if only for a while.

So she left her garden in the care of a friend while she set out in search of peace. Perhaps a man could give her that peace, she mused. Perhaps another kind of work. Perhaps a new philosophy, a religious experience, advice from a wise, old woman. Perhaps just playing at being a child again.

Becky traveled far and wide in search of her peace. And the garden grew weeds in her absence. No friend, however well meaning, knows a garden like its caretaker. And each time Becky returned home from one of her trips, she dreaded looking at her patch of land. What small peace she had found in her travels disappeared when she viewed the condition of her beloved garden plants.

There is no peace for those whose gardens are in disorder, however thin the soil.

This story was written for a charming young lady who was considering flight from her marital garden. Whenever possible, it is best to put one's garden in order before walking away from it. In her case working on the garden eliminated the need for walking away.

We all get tired of difficult work at times. We all feel the warm pull of peace and security and time-out from responsibilities that might come from escape of one sort or another. Long-term fulfillment for adults comes from being who we are—adults. There is a difference between short-term relief and walking out on our responsibilities.

A Wet and Dry Relationship

Hachi was a Siamese cat with all the aloofness and pride of breeding that such cats have. Hachi would sit quietly grooming herself until satisfied that her appearance was perfect. Then she would rise, arch her back, and stretch luxuriously before stalking into the next room to parade herself in front of the mirror.

Hachi played a variety of games to amuse herself during the long hours during the day while her master was at work. For example, she pretended there was a mouse in the bedroom. Carefully, silently she would pad her way toward the imaginary mouse (ordinarily, it was a bedroom slipper) and then pounce upon it, digging her claws into the terry cloth with mock ferocity. In that elegant apartment building no mouse had appeared for years. But it was fun to pretend.

Hachi's master lived alone in the apartment with his pet cat. They had a peaceful relationship unruffled by strong emotions. Hachi considered it convenient to have someone around to provide food and keep their living space clean. The man found it pleasant to have some living creature waiting when he returned from work. They respected each other's moods, gave each other plenty of space, and got along well.

Strangely, the only time Hachi wanted to curl up and be petted, the only time when she wanted closeness and warm affection was just before her master went off to work each morning. Then

Hachi would rub herself against his trousers, purr and stretch, and try to look available and adorable. Even more strangely, when the man began to respond to Hachi's show of affection, when he reached down to pick her up and run his fingers through her short fur, Hachi would suddenly panic and run to hide behind the couch in the den.

"What an odd cat," the man thought each morning and smiled. Then off he would go to work.

At night when he returned he would set out fresh water and cat food, then prepare his own simple supper. Hachi would appear shyly in the doorway to the den. Her eyes would follow his movements for a while as if checking to see whether he was angry with her. Then she would cross the kitchen to her food dish, ignoring his presence with a great show of indifference.

Why Hachi felt this ambivalence about closeness her master never knew. Why she approached him just as he was about to leave, then fled when he responded to her feline charms, he couldn't ask. Perhaps he thought that if he waited long enough, Hachi would change. Perhaps he was satisfied just to live with an unusual roommate.

At any rate, they lived together for years. In time her master's patience was rewarded with more and more affection. But they remained to the end a rather strange couple demonstrating an appreciation for, as the Japanese would say, the wet and the dry.

The life of this "couple" proceeded smoothly and harmoniously because of mutual acceptance (which goes beyond tolerance), mutual service, and the ability to wait. How different their lives would have been if Hachi's master demanded more of a demonstration of appreciation and affection or if Hachi demanded her master's attention throughout the day.

The Hiding Place

Once upon a time there was a lovely young princess whose charms attracted suitors from all over the realm. She wanted none of the young men who came seeking her hand, however. Perhaps no one, even in this fantastic kingdom, could live up to the ideal she envisioned. Her father, the king, grew impatient with his daughter's habit of turning away those who came to court her even when she had no reason.

The clever princess decided on a plan that would at once satisfy her father and herself. She announced publicly that she would marry the first young man who could hide himself in a place where she couldn't find him. Now, the princess possessed magical abilities that allowed her to travel anywhere in an instant. She could use her magic to track down anyone who undertook the challenge.

Many came, and all of them failed to find a hidden place where the princess couldn't find them. From the ocean depths to the tops of mountains they hid. But none remained successfully concealed.

One day an eager young knight, Sir Wakamono, was riding along the main highway headed for the castle and his chance to try to win the hand of the princess. An old woman cried from the side of the road, "Please, Sir Knight, could you give me a lift to the next town? I've grown weary from my long journey and haven't the strength to continue on by foot."

Although Sir Wakamono had been taught never to pick up hitchhikers, he could see no harm in giving this old lady a ride. So he reached down and swung her up onto the saddle behind him. As they rode along, he told the tale of his quest. As frequently happens in these circumstances, the old woman was a fairy godmother in disguise. In gratitude for the knight's kindness she offered a magical belt buckle and some hints about hiding where the princess wouldn't be likely to search. The belt buckle could be used to transport the knight instantly to any place in the kingdom. It was designed to become obsolete after three uses (actually, the odd-sized batteries were drained after three pulls of their energy and couldn't be replaced).

The next day Knight Wakamono presented himself at court and undertook the set task of concealing himself where the princess couldn't find him. The fairy godmother's advice had been to use the magic buckle to hide himself, on first try, in the princess's own heart.

"People know their own hearts least of all. The princess never thinks to examine it closely," he had been told. "She won't find you there."

So the knight fingered his buckle and wished to conceal himself in the princess's heart. But he found that her heart was already so filled with thoughts about herself that there was no room there for him to hide.

Sir Wakamono tried next to hide in her eyes, thinking, "She cannot see me if I burrow into the source of her vision." Again he rubbed the magic buckle. But, alas, her eyes, too, were filled with images of herself. He could find no space to secrete himself.

Recognizing that he had been outsmarted, Sir Wakamono used his final stroke of the transistorized buckle to save the long journey home. He was transported instantly back to his town.

Such is the tale of Sir Wakamono. The princess continued to find those who tried to hide from her. As time passed, those who arrived to seek her hand grew fewer and fewer in number. She defeated them all, and after a while no one seemed to care. She won, but she began to realize that she had lost.

Oh, yes, and Sir Wakamono learned that, sometimes, even wise old godmothers are wrong.

DAVID K. REYNOLDS

There is a related Naikan story about a suitor who hides in the princess's heart, where she cannot find him. That story makes the point that few people take the time to examine what they have stored away in their hearts over the years. Naikan self-reflection involves an entire week of examining the past as it has been coded in the heart.

The story here adds reflections on self-centeredness, the source of seeing, winning and losing, and expectations about the infallibility of wisdom, among others.

High Rider

Phil's younger brother, Billy, was seven years old, but he weighed less than thirty pounds. From the time of Billy's birth the lad was unusually small, physically deformed, and mildly disabled mentally. Phil was a strapping youth of nineteen, one of the best distance runners in the state.

The two brothers were very close. In fact, Phil trained and ran his races with Billy riding on his shoulders. Their odd practice began when Phil took Billy for a ride as a weight to strengthen his legs during practice for an upcoming marathon. Billy loved the feel of the wind streaming past his face. He laughed with delight from the very first time he climbed aboard. Billy learned to grip his brother's head tightly while straddling Phil's neck and to maintain silence as his brother's feet bounded over the courses. The smile never left Billy's face during a run. In time, around the state meets, people came to expect to see Phil running with Billy astride his shoulders.

A coach once persuaded Phil to run without his brother. Phil discovered that he couldn't run the same distances in the same times when he ran alone. His balance seemed strained, off.

"I get bored doing it alone. I start noticing how tired I am. Billy and I never talk when we run together." (Phil never considered that he was "carrying" Billy; they were "running together.") "But, still, he's with me and that makes a difference."

DAVID K. REYNOLDS

The state ten-kilometer run was only a month away when Phil asked Billy to run with him again. And Billy refused!

"You wouldn't let me run with you all last week. I'm no different from you. I can run by myself, too. I'll enter the race on my own!" Billy voiced his resentment and walked away.

"Fine," his father told him a few minutes later, "Run."

"Well, I can't right now. I'm not in good shape. And, maybe, I'll need special shoes or something." Billy slowed down a bit.

"Make a list of what you need, and I'll get it for you," his father said evenly. "You have a month to get ready for the ten-kilometer run, Billy."

The lad thought for a few moments.

"All right, I'm not the same as Phil. I need Phil if I'm going to run."

"Billy," his brother grinned, walking up from behind, "I'm the one who needs you. Just can't get my stride without you."

That year the race officials had to give two first-place prizes.

We aren't all born with the same capabilities. We all depend on the abilities of others for our survival and satisfaction. Given the way social status is defined in our society, it may be easy to forget that we need readers, patients, students, and clerks as much as we need authors, physicians, teachers, and managers.

A "handicap" permits the opportunity for a mutual exchange like that in the story. Billy was both buoy and burden—just like the rest of us.

Look-Alikes

Nita woke up one morning to find that everyone's face resembled her own. What a surprise! Her mother and her brother, the postlady and the delivery boy, the president and the crossing guard—everyone seemed to have Nita's face sitting on their necks. What's more, Nita could detect her mannerisms, her faults, her sorrows, and hopes in everyone around her.

At first Nita was frightened by all this similarity. When she helped her mother take off the pillowcases for the laundry, it almost seemed as though she were helping herself. When she thanked her mother's friend for the fresh-baked cookie, it was almost like thanking herself.

Amazingly, when she went to scold her younger sister, Nita found herself softening her words because the little girl put on Nita's own teary eyes and buckling eyebrows. Anyway, the little girl was only doing something Nita herself had done at that age. It felt as though she were scolding a mirror.

Nita had to learn how to differentiate people all over again. There were small differences about their facial features that helped distinguish them. Furthermore, there were differences in their clothing and sizes and surroundings. But sometimes she made mistakes, and always others were reminders of who she herself was.

Nita grew up to be one of the most beloved people in her

DAVID K. REYNOLDS

town. She kept insisting that everything she did for someone else was not really different from doing the same thing for herself, that anyone else's worries really felt like her own. She kept saying she was the most selfish person of anyone she knew. And she truly, truly meant her words.

Still, people loved her. Everyone who knew her felt close to her.

Note the difference here between Nita's orientation and the Golden Rule. The two shouldn't be confused. It is important to be able to see ourselves in others to achieve a certain level of constructive growth.

The Mango Tree

Once there was a mango tree, grown full in the tropical sun. Each day it endured the heat and still provided shade for those who rested under it. It produced abundant fruit, though some of it was too high for some folks to reach. The highest fruit looked so tasty that some people tried to throw rocks at it to knock it to the ground so that they could sample it. Some birds nested in the tree. They came and went at their own convenience, safe in the strongest of storms.

In time, the tree died. Still, its remains were used by many creatures as a home and resource. Throughout its existence it just remained a mango tree, doing what mango trees do. It didn't wish it were a pampered citrus tree or a flowering cherry tree. It took the heat and storms that came its way and stood in there, useful. What more can you ask of a mango tree?

What more can we ask of anyone?

I wrote this story one day after visiting an abandoned sugarcane camp to pick mangoes. The old camp houses at Camp Seven were falling down; the dirt roads were in poor shape, but the mango trees stood there as they had stood for years and years. The camp members of earlier times still returned to pick and enjoy the mangoes (picked half-ripe and eaten with soy sauce). Those sturdy mango trees just kept on doing their duty—abandoned, alone, they endured Kauai's heat and storms and put out there fruit.

DAVID K. REYNOLDS

The Mirror

Once upon a time there was a young boy who stood before the mirror every day before going outside to meet his friends. When he reached the age of nine, he began to notice that the top of his head was beginning to disappear from the mirror. By the time he was ten, his entire forehead had disappeared. By eleven, his nose had disappeared. And when he reached his twelfth birthday, his face had disappeared entirely from the mirror.

This experience worried him somewhat. The only reassuring fact was that he could recognize his body in the mirror, though his body, too, seemed to be changing. Still, he hadn't entirely vanished.

When he shared his puzzlement with some of the adults around him, he got various pieces of advice. His mother recommended that he kneel to find himself in the mirror. His father suggested that he bow himself over to rediscover his face. One uncle told him there was something wrong with the mirror. An aunt told him to put books under the mirror. His grandfather told him he had outgrown the mirror and needn't spend so much time looking at himself in it anyway.

Who and what are your mirrors? How has your reflection changed over time? What meaning lies within the varieties of advice for finding yourself?

Soft and Easy

The mud people of Planet Three were just that—they were made of mud. Their planet circled a sun that was sometimes hot and near, sometimes cool and distant. Some days the sun would shine; some days the rain would pour.

Put simply, there were two kinds of mud people. Some of them would work long and hard even on hot days, when the sun's orbit swung it near the planet. They received ridicule for their long hours of toil on these days. It wasn't, after all, economically necessary to work so hard. Mud people need very little in the way of creature comforts. Those who stayed out in the sun to labor on such hot days found their bodies baked hard as stone. They lost a certain amount of social status by their tough, dark appearance.

The other category of mud people worked only on cloudy, cool days. Mostly, they worked when they felt like working. They were known for taking a lot of time getting ready to work after they arrived in the fields, and they started getting ready to go home well before dark. They were respected and paid handsomely by mud-folk society. Their moist softness was a sign of luxury, beauty, and prestige. They prospered.

Until the rainy season came.

Anyone who consistently takes the soft and easy course turns out soft and easy.

DAVID K. REYNOLDS

No Parking

Clara wanted her old energy back, and her old figure, and her old high spirits (at least, she wanted her memory's version of them). Drinking and a failed marriage and the kids grown and gone and the sameness about her work and her evenings and, oh, a lot of other tragedies had conspired to bring her to the point of wanting to park her life in a permanent garage. And Clara was only forty-five.

Her feet walked her to the Golden Gate Bridge, where she looked for a reasonable place to jump. A cable man noticed her, suspected her intent, and walked her back to the end of the bridge. He hailed a cab for Clara, paid the cabbie, and sent her home—home to the sameness again. A friend at work noticed that Clara hadn't shown up for two days. She went to Clara's apartment and discovered her lying comatose on the bed with bottles and pills scattered about. Fortunately, Clara had only double-parked.

The hospital called the kids. They came and cried and told Clara they loved her. But in ten days it was back to the sameness again.

Then, one afternoon Clara went to a fortune-teller, who told her she didn't have to drive her old-model life anymore. She had the right to trade in her life on a new model. In fact, she could have the color and interior of her choice.

"Wow," thought Clara aloud, "I thought that God or Karma or something like that selected models and colors and engines for us."

"No," corrected the fortune-teller. "They provide some raw materials to work with and some of the scenery you drive through, but the choice of cars is yours. You have been driving your own special model all along."

"Interesting idea," said Clara. "What do I need to do to get my order in on a new model?"

"You design your lifemobile with your actions," she was told. "You have the option at any time to modify the design."

"But I'm used to doing things a certain way. It would be hard to change."

"Do you like the model you've been driving recently?"

"Are you kidding? It barely runs at all."

"Then you have to redesign it. You have to change what you do. Is Clara your first name? Have you a middle name?"

"May."

"May it is, then. Use the name May from now on to remind yourself of your new sedan. Maybe May would like to drive back to the bridge and thank the fellow who sent Clara home in the cab."

Well, May did just that. What's more, there's an unexpected twist to her story: She's engaged to that fellow now. She bought a gift for her friend at work, then changed jobs. May lost twenty-five pounds, runs two miles every other day, and eats more carefully than when she was Clara. May enrolled in a continuing-education class at a local college. She's into writing, I hear. And in the driver's seat of life.

May's car runs pretty well these days; it only needs an occasional tune-up. May never thinks of permanently parking it. Once in a while the sad, old Clara pops up. Then May laughs and reminds her, "I thought I told you to wait in the car."

We can write anew our lives through changed present behavior. Sometimes it is helpful to change our environment to remind ourselves of our new purposes. A new name, a redecorated kitchen, a change of scenery, a different job, joining a new club, new friends— these aren't the whole solution, but they can function to keep reminding us of what we need to do to create our new identities.

Polly's Cracker

Polly Glotz and her husband divorced after quite a few years of marriage. The way Polly saw it, he had found a younger woman and ran off. Polly hated him with the special hatred reserved for a woman who expects her man to love her in the same way she loves him and discovers otherwise.

The divorce settlement allowed Polly to keep the couple's parrot, a young bird of only a year. Polly devoted many hours in the next weeks and months teaching the bird to rasp vile expletives whenever the name of her ex-husband was mentioned. The parrot, of course, understood nothing of what it was saying or why. It just mimicked the foul words it heard over and over again.

Polly wondered why no one else appeared to care much for her parrot. Friends seemed to avoid visiting her home. They never went near the birdcage. The truth was simple. No one else wanted to hear the repetitious and vicious chatter about her former husband. It was old history, the breakup. Why not get on with other things?

A few old friends felt sorry for Polly. More felt sorry for the parrot. Still, they didn't come to visit very often.

This is a story written for a person who was turning the children in her custody into parrots like Polly's.

Priorities

He was balding and in his fifties, but as he sat on the stage behind the cloth-draped table, he looked like a little boy. The microphone was the only accessory on the table. He looked at it distastefully from time to time as he responded to the questions and comments from the audience. He had come all this way, and the glory had no taste in his mouth—his wife was dying.

If we must give him a name, let it be Avery Mann, for reasons that are obvious. There is some of this man in all of us. He struggled and produced and endured until he was at the top of his profession. He had given his major address on biogenetics, he had received the medal that signified highest achievement in his field, and now he faced the questions and admiration of colleagues and reporters.

And his wife was dying of cancer. His wife was dying of cancer.

It isn't unusual in these times of competition that a man sacrifices his family for the professional success he dearly desires. It isn't that he makes the sacrifice consciously and with intention. Rather, like Professor Mann, he makes small choices about when and where he will work, about what he includes in his topics of conversation, about how he spends his evenings and weekends, choices about where his energy and attention will be focused during vacations, about who receives his gifts and why. Without any

DAVID K. REYNOLDS

real recognition of what was happening so gradually, Mann found himself an outsider in his own family, a sort of tolerated stranger who paid his way and caused only a little inconvenience.

Perhaps his wife could have come to love Mann again if he had shown her the attention and courtesy of their courtship days. But he found no time for such frills as he climbed the academic ladder, carefully watching those above and below him.

Only when the physician telephoned to tell him the diagnosis and the need for exploratory surgery did he stop to look for the ladder from which his wife had fallen. He had great difficulty making it out in the distance.

Their daughter would give birth to their first grandchild in another five months. Mann worried that Anna wouldn't live to see the new life. There was so much he could control in his professional life, so many people would move at his bidding, so much research money would be redirected at his whim. Yet there was absolutely nothing he or the physicians could to do to prevent the ultimate victory of the spreading tumors.

Avery's dilemma isn't unusual in these times. Of what good is the fancy house when there is no one to view it? Of what good is the outrageous salary when there is no one to spend it on? He climbed so fast that he left his family behind. They couldn't keep up.

We forget to ask ourselves, "What is it for?" We get caught up in the succeeding itself, while its purpose drops from awareness. Again, reality reminds us, sometimes painfully, of our distraction from purpose. Avery recognized the reminder rather late in the game. His wife's illness was not the only clue reality sent him, of course. But it was a message so strong he couldn't ignore it.

Pushaway

Beverly's son, Peter, had a rare eating disorder. He was hungry all the time. What is more, his body used every calorie of every bit of food Beverly prepared for him. Peter never became fat; he never became full. From morning until night Beverly was busy cooking for her son and serving him meal after meal.

Some young men naturally outgrow this disorder as they pass through adolescence. But there was no guarantee that Peter would do so. Year after year Beverly grew more tired. More and more she turned to fast-food kitchens to feed her son so that she could have some time for herself.

When she had a few hours free, she fled from the kitchen to her parents' home. At first she spent her time there complaining of the terrible burden her son had become. But the complaints solved nothing. Furthermore, she felt hungry herself. Increasingly, as the years passed, she spent her time at the dining table eating her mother's food.

"I am so busy preparing Peter's food, I have no time to eat myself. How much I need the food you make for me," she told her mother tearfully.

"You never talk to me anymore," her mother complained. "You walk in the front door and head for the refrigerator. And, frankly, I'm getting tired of it. You are a grown woman, now I have other things to do besides feeding you."

As soon as Beverly would leave the house, her mother would run to her husband's room and cry about the change that had come over their daughter.

"All you do is cry these days," he remonstrated her. He became so unhappy that he began to see a psychotherapist who was grossly overweight.

And so it goes.

Demands produce demands produce demands in endless cycles. Needs produce needs produce needs in the same cycles. Who can give without taking? But how many take without giving?

It Feels So Right It Must Be Wrong

Sir Ronald was the bravest knight in the kingdom. He was also the most chivalrous, the most handsome, and the purest of heart: a certified dreamboat. When he met Maiden Gwendolyn his heart boomed with certainty that this lovely lass would someday be his bride.

He courted her in proper and gallant style. As though it had been meant to be from the start, he easily won her heart. The date of their wedding was set. All the court looked forward to celebrating the joining of this perfectly paired couple.

All seemed to be going well in this divinely orchestrated concerto of love. Why, then, did Sir Ronald feel so uneasy?

"Dissatisfied?" his best friend, Sir Linus, could scarcely believe his ears. "How can you be dissatisfied? You are about to marry the most wondrous woman in the realm!"

"Oh, it's not *her*. She is perfection itself. The problem lies within *me*. It all feels too smooth, too ideal. It cannot be right to marry in this way. I feel guilty, endangered, restless."

"Every ordinary man feels jittery before making this commitment," Sir Linus reassured him. "But I wouldn't have expected it of you."

"No, no. It is more than that," exclaimed Sir Ronald. "How can I explain it. It must be wrong, this thing I am about to do."

"Why?"

"I cannot say. It . it . . . it seems so natural, so easy. It *has* to be wrong."

"It seems so *natural* that it must be *wrong*? You are a fool, my friend." Sir Linus shook his head and clapped his gloved hand on Sir Ronald's shoulder. "Perhaps you should talk to the priest tonight. The wedding is less than a week away."

Sir Ronald made arrangements to meet with the priest late that night. When all was quiet within the castle walls, he stole quietly into the sanctuary, where a single candle burned.

The wedding took place without a hitch. What a lovely pair of newlyweds! Sir Ronald was beaming. As they glided out beneath the arch of crossed swords, there was no doubt, no advice, no priest.

We see both extremes in our era: those who follow the it-feels-so-good-it-must-be-right philosophy and those who follow the it-feels-so-right-it-must-be-wrong orientation. Both extremes are, well, extreme. What advice did the priest give Sir Ronald?

Runaway

Once upon a time there was a little girl named Georgette. She knew all the answers to the questions her teachers asked at school. She tried very hard to be a nice little girl. She wanted everyone to like her.

Georgette was surprised and hurt to find that some of the children in her class didn't like her at all. And she was even more surprised and hurt when her brother ran away from home.

"I try very hard to be smart and kind and good to everyone," she thought. "Some people understand how hard I work at being lovable. My teachers seem to understand. Why don't some of my classmates recognize my effort and love me? Why did my favorite brother run away from me? Maybe there is something wrong with me. Maybe there is something about me that frightens people away."

So Georgette took special charm classes and difficult courses in school and tried to improve herself even more. In one of her special classes the teacher kept saying that children are just fine as they are. Georgette had trouble understanding how the dirty-faced, snotty-nosed tease who sat next to her could be fine just as he was. When she finally figured out why he was beautiful, she also understood that she was beautiful, too, no matter who didn't like her, no matter who ran away.

And those who run away are just fine as they are, too.

∗   ∗   ∗

This tale was written for a physician who was training for certification in Morita guidance. Like most of us, she worked hard at achieving her goals and being likable. She, too, felt the hurt of rejection at times, a hurt that caused her to have the predictable doubts about herself.

This is a tale about acceptance—of others as they are, of ourselves as we are. Acceptance may not eliminate the self-doubts, but the self-doubts become acceptable, too.

Seeing Clearly

A crowd had gathered around the old shell-game huckster. The pale man with a moustache was rapidly taking in the dollars, one at a time, as the guesses failed. His eyes seemed everywhere at once—sizing up the next victim, watching for police, maneuvering the bean beneath the three paper cups.

Lenny had just arrived in the city. He noticed the crowd and drifted over to have a look at what was attracting the people. After all, he wanted to learn about city life, so he needed to find out what drew the attention of city folks. Lenny was only fourteen, but he made up for inexperience with alertness and a solid grasp of the fact that he was on his own.

"What's going on here?" he asked a middle-aged man in a faded pinstriped suit.

"It's the old shell game, Son. Never seen it before?"

"No, never have. How does it work?" Lenny wondered.

"It's simple. That guy hides a bean under one of the cups, and you try to guess which one it's under. If you win, you get your dollar back and one of his."

"That seems pretty easy," said Lenny. "Now it's under the cup on the left."

Lenny was right.

"Now it's under the middle cup."

Again, he was right.

DAVID K. REYNOLDS

"Now it's under the left cup again."

And, again, Lenny was right on the money.

Mr. Pinstripe Suit was impressed. He staked Lenny to a few dollars and watched his money triple itself before the huckster moved on to easier pickings.

"That's quite a talent you have," he praised Lenny as he divided the winnings with the lad.

"But I only said what I saw."

"To see clearly, and to let others know what you see is the highest art." Mr. Pinstripe Suit's face was quite serious for a moment. Then he grinned and disappeared into the crowd.

Seeing reality as it is seems to be more difficult for some people to approach than for others. Communicating clearly about the reality we see is no easy task for most of us. But the gains from our efforts in these directions make our exertions worthwhile.

Terrarium

The peperomia plant had been placed in a terrarium with a completely enclosed environment. The plant struggled over the years to grow and fill the terrarium's space. As the years passed, it managed to expand and to press against the top and sides of its glass enclosure. The plant discovered that it must either break out of the limits of its immediate environment or die. There was no more room to grow, no more room to be active, no more room to struggle. The peperomia plant had won all the available battles; it had succeeded marvelously. So it faced either death or the push through to a wider world.

Successful people, too, have moments of despair. Sometimes the cause seems to be an unwillingness to risk breaking through to new circumstances with new challenges. These people don't need to change the unwillingness, but they need to act on the need to break through.

DAVID K. REYNOLDS

Wings

In a castle town in Europe there lived three brothers. From the time they were old enough to go to school, they were obsessed with the desire to fly. The hunting falcons glided so effortlessly, then darted at their prey with power and agility. The kites tugged toward freedom above the castle walls. How wonderful it would be to soar in unbounded space! In time, the brothers became adults.

Karl, the eldest, studied birds. He knew the structures of their wings and feathers intimately. He dreamed and dreamed of being a bird. But he never flew.

Kurt, the second son, studied himself. He learned in detail the physiological conditions that prevented him from flying. He turned inward and brooded about his limitations. He never flew.

Kevin, the youngest, studied methods—the methods of science, engineering, mechanical crafting, business economics. He built models and prototypes and, at last, a flying machine. He flew.

When Kevin asked his brothers to share the seats in his flying machine, they refused. A noisy, dangerous mechanical contraption could find no place in Karl's dreams. Kurt felt no confidence that the device could carry him with all his structural weakness.

Only Kevin flew. He raced the falcons and circled the kites. Then he went on to invent other marvelous devices.

There is nothing wrong with dreaming, unless we only dream. There is nothing wrong with introspection, unless that is all we do. It is important to learn methods for effective action. Whether the methods are psychological or political or artistic or mechanical, they provide us with tools for moving beyond mental wheelspinning.

Our method emphasizes practical learning for practical living. When we have mastered the appropriate methods and have fulfilled one dream, we can move on to tackling the next.

Western Logic:
It's Gotta Be Yes or No

Mr. Soko is a strange man of about fifty years old with eyes like a baby's. He dresses respectably but always seems a bit out of fashion. Yet he is a popular figure in the media, for he can be counted on to say something unusual and newsworthy. On this morning he settled himself in the modern swivel chair provided on the set of a television interview program.

Two aggressive host-interviewers probed his opinions about the upcoming talks on nuclear disarmament. One of the interviewers was in favor of the talks, and one of the interviewers was opposed to them. The first mentioned some of the arguments supporting the talks.

"Yes, you have a point there," replied Mr. Soko.

The second interviewer countered with arguments against the talks.

"You certainly seem to know what you're talking about," commented Mr. Soko.

The first rebutted.

"What you have to say sounds good to me," Mr. Soko remarked in response.

The second countered.

"I wouldn't disagree with that point."

"That makes sense."

"Couldn't have put it better myself."

At last the first host expressed his exasperation. "But Mr. Soko, how can you agree with both of us? Either the nuclear disarmament talks are useful or they're not. You can't have it both ways."

"Undoubtedly, you are right again. I find nothing wrong with your logic on that matter."

"Then which is right?" the host pushed.

"Yes, which indeed?"

"Aren't you willing to commit yourself to one position or the other?" the second host probed.

"Why should I?" the guest wanted to know.

"Because you must have some views on the matter of disarmament talks."

"Yes, I have."

"Well, which stand do you agree with?"

"Must I choose one or the other?"

"Yes, of course, that is the purpose of this interview. You must choose."

"Excuse me," Mr. Soko said mildly. And he stood up and walked off the set.

Needless to say, the cameraman wondered what he should do as the guest's back disappeared from the lighted set. The two hosts, however, quickly recovered and filled the rest of the airtime with a lively discussion of Mr. Soko's unexpected behavior.

Pro or con, true or false, scientific or unscientific, East or West, good or bad, capitalism or communism—our thinking gets directed toward exclusive dichotomies. The real world is far too complicated to allow such simplistic on-or-off thinking. Formal logic, binary computer circuits, and the like are creations of human thought. In those restricted areas dichotomous evaluations are necessary and proper. But when we talk about a college education or psychoanalysis or tonight's dinner, a one-word evaluation makes little sense.

Nevertheless, with all this complexity, we must act.

References

Blyth, R. H. *Zen and Zen Classics,* ed. Frederick Franck. New York: Vintage, 1978.

Cook, Francis Dojun. *How to Raise an Ox.* Los Angeles: Center Publications, 1978.

Dogen, *Record of Things Heard,* trans. Thomas Cleary. Boulder, Colo.: Prajna Press, 1980.

Doi, Takeo. *The Anatomy of Dependence,* trans. John Bestor. Tokyo: Kodansha, 1973.

Iwai, Hiroshi, and Reynolds, David K. "Morita Therapy: The Views From the West." *American Journal of Psychiatry* 126(7), 1031–1036, 1970.

Kondo, Akihisa. "Morita Therapy: A Japanese Therapy for Neurosis." *American Journal of Psychoanalysis* 13, 31–37, 1953.

Kora, Takehisa. "Morita Therapy." *International Journal of Psychiatry* 1(4), 611–640, 1965.

Kora, Takehisa, and Ohara, Kenshiro. "Morita Therapy." *Psychology Today* 6(10), 63–68, 1973.

LaFleur, William. *The Karma of Words.* Berkeley, Calif.: University of California Press, 1983.

Laing, R. D., and Esterson, A. *Sanity, Madness, and the Family.* New York: Penguin, 1964.

Magnusson, David, ed. *Toward a Psychology of Situations.* Hillsdale, N. J.: Lawrence Erlbaum, 1981.

Miura, Momoshige, and Usa, Shin-ichi. "Morita Therapy." *Psychologia* 13(1), 18–34. 1970.

Ohara, Kenshiro, and Reynolds, David K. "Changing Methods in Morita Psychotherapy." *International Journal of Social Psychiatry* 14(4), 305–310, 1968.

Reynolds, David K. *Morita Psychotherapy*. Berkeley, Calif.: Univeristy of California Press, 1976.

———. "Naikan Therapy—An Experiential View." *International Journal of Social Psychiatry* 23(4), 252–264, 1977.

———. *The Quiet Therapies*. Honolulu: University of Hawaii Press, 1980.

———. "Morita Psychotherapy." *Handbook of Innovative Psychotherapies*, ed. R. Corsini. New York: Wiley, 1981.

———. "Naikan Therapy." In *Handbook of Innovative Psychotherapies*, ed. R. Corsini. New York: Wiley, 1981.

———. *Naikan Psychotherapy: Meditation for Self-development*. Chicago: University of Chicago Press, 1983.

———. *Constructive Living*. Honolulu: University of Hawaii Press, 1984.

———. *Playing Ball on Running Water*. New York: Quill, 1984.

———. *Even in Summer the Ice Doesn't Melt*. New York: Quill, 1986.

———, and Norman L. Farberow, *Suicide: Inside and Out*. Berkeley, Calif.: University of California Press, 1976.

——— and Norman L. Farberow. *The Family Shadow*. Berkeley, Calif.: University of California Press, 1981.

———, and Kiefer, C. W. "Cultural Adaptability as an Attribute of Therapies: The Case of Morita Psychotherapy." *Culture, Medicine, and Psychiatry* 1, 395–412. 1977.

"The Staff Program." *Zen Bow* 9 (3, 4), 65–67, 1977.

Suzuki, Daisetz Teitaro. *The Training of the Zen Buddhist Monk*. New York, University Books, 1965.

Suzuki, Tomonori, and Suzuki, Ryu. "Morita Therapy." In *Psychosomatic Medicine*, ed. Eric D. Wittkower and Hector Warnes. New York: Harper and Row, 1977.

Suzuki, Tomonori, and Suzuki, Ryu. "The Effectiveness of In-patient Morita Therapy." *Psychiatric Quarterly* 53(3), 201–213, 1981.

Trungpa, Chogyam. *Glimpses of Abhidharma*. Boulder, Colo., Prajna Press, 1975.

Usa, Genyu, and Usa, Shin-ichi. "A Case of a Nun Who Suffered From Visionary Obsessions of Snakes, Treated by Morita Therapy." *Psychologia* 1, 226–228, 1958.

Watts, Alan. *The Essence of Alan Watts*. Millbrae, Calif., Celestial Arts, 1974.

"Work." *Zen Bow* 9 (3, 4), 59–64, 1977.

About the Author

David K. Reynolds, Ph.D., has been on the faculty of UCLA, the University of Southern California School of Medicine, and the University of Houston. He is director of the ToDo Institute in Los Angeles and co-director of the Health Center Pacific in Maui. He travels among Constructive Living centers in Los Angeles, Hawaii, Tokyo, and New York, lecturing training professionals, and conducting a small private practice in English and in Japanese.

Dr. Reynolds is the author of more than fifteen books published in the United States and Japan. Recent titles include *Playing Ball on Running Water, Even in Summer the Ice Doesn't Melt, Constructive Living, Naikan Psychotherapy,* and *The Quiet Therapies.*